PRAISE FOR

NO MORE HOLDING BACK

"With wit and candor and a responsible use of Scripture, Kat Armstrong makes a winsome case for women in ministry. What the church needs most is not loud and shrill voices, nor does it need arguments rooted in Western liberalism's sense of justice. What it most needs is gifted women to use their gifts for the glory of God in the church. Barriers are broken down not by activism but by the beauty of God's Spirit speaking to God's people through women who are gifted to speak. Kat Armstrong is one of those gifts using her gifts to open Scripture for all of us."

—Rev. Canon Dr. Scot McKnight
Professor of New Testament, Northern Seminary

"Kat is one of my favorite Bible teachers, and I've been supporting her work through Polished for years. She inspires me every time I hear her speak, and, finally, we have her grace-filled teaching in a book! Every woman needs her words, especially at such a time like this."

—Catherine Giudici Lowe
Reality TV personality
Founder/CEO of LoweCo. and LoweCo.ncierge

"Kat Armstrong is the woman to write this book. She lives this message every day by investing in women and elevating them with more diligence and zeal than just about anyone I know. Being a woman in leadership is lonely work, but *No More Holding Back* fires a shot across the bow of that isolation. If you are yearning for a friend who understands the challenges of leadership as well as a fellow soldier who will rally you to more, this book is for you!"

—Sharon Hodde Miller
Author of *Free of Me: Why Life Is Better When It's Not About You*

"Kat is a brilliant Bible teacher and a ferocious cheerleader for women. I underlined so much of my book and said out loud 'You go, girl' more times than I can count! This book will challenge you, encourage you, and inspire you to do all the great things that God has prepared in advance for you to do. On behalf of all the women now and in the generations to come, I say thank you, Kat, for writing these words for us."

–Jamie Ivey
Bestselling author of *If You Only Knew* and host
of *The Happy Hour with Jamie Ivey*

"What a joy to read *No More Holding Back*. Its message is on target: women are gifted by God to love and serve him fully. Men and women are to honor God together. Created as a team to image God, we live out our calling best when we encourage each other in growth and ministry. In tandem, we are strong. Sometimes that means dealing with misconceptions directly as Kat does and then moving forward without holding back. Read this book and let's cheer one another on to a deeper walk, better cooperation, and more effective ministry together with God."

–Darrell L. Bock
Senior research professor of New Testament
studies, Dallas Theological Seminary

"*No More Holding Back* is an invitation for women to shift from risk managers to risk engagers. . . . Kat's transparency and vulnerability serve to unearth the type of courageous surrender that results in us rising up and stepping out for such a time as this. Every page is part of a supernatural recruiting session calling you into your life mission, your true purpose, and your born identity. It's a charge for women of faith to stop hiding out in God's heart and start being what he always intended—women of wisdom and worth who operate without approval and without apology. These women are indeed dangerous, and that's exactly what heaven is after."

–Marshawn Evans Daniels
Godfidence Coach, TV personality, reinvention strategist for women
Founder of SheProfits.com

"Kat is a gifted communicator, and in this, her first book, her skills are on full display. Her passion for ministry, compassion for people, confidence in the gospel, and commitment to discipleship are contagious. . . . This book is challenging at points, even confrontational, but with a winsome and gracious tone. Kat really does believe that women, and men, should be emboldened to love God and love others and, in so doing, push back against the prevailing power of karma that rules this world. Karma enslaves and kills. Grace sets us free and gives life; it really is a thought that will change the world."

—Glenn R. Kreider
Professor of theological studies, Dallas Theological Seminary
Author, *God with Us*

"The assumption within Christian circles is that for women and girls silence is golden, deference and submission are supreme virtues, and less is more. . . . Kat Armstrong draws from her own struggles with these confining, cautionary messages to summon her sisters in Christ to stop holding back. Her passionate call to shed these hindrances and press on to love God freely with all our hearts, minds, souls, and strength is crucial reading for the whole church!"

—Carolyn Custis James
Author of *Half the Church: Recapturing God's Global Vision for Women* and *Finding God in the Margins*

"I have sat under Kat Armstrong's memorable teaching at a women's event, and it is clear God created and formed her to be full of faith, passionate, articulate, and one who handles God's word with knowledge and skill. She brings these same elements onto the pages of her fantastic book. Reading *No More Holding Back* in my car, I held back the strong urge to jump on the hood and yell, 'Yes! Everyone needs to read this book!' Kat's book is going to set women free to live and serve God. Highly recommend!"

—Vivian Mabuni
Speaker and author of *Open Hands, Willing Heart: Discover the Joy of Saying Yes to God*

"*No More Holding Back* had me jumping out of my seat with praise! Now is the time to look into our rich heritage of faith to find the women of the Bible risking it all to follow after Christ. Kat is someone I deeply respect and I know her words will be an encouragement to you."

—Tasha Morrison
President and founder of Be The Bridge

"Y'all, listen: Kat has a way of drawing us into her story and experience with authenticity, humor, and straight talk about the Bible. This will be my go-to resource for anyone looking to elevate women's voices in the church and to see women everywhere flourish in their gifts. *No More Holding Back* is a game changer!"

—Jessica Honegger
Bestselling author of *Imperfect Courage*
Founder of Noonday Collection

"Ladies, come *on*! In the first few pages I found myself clapping and shouting, 'Preach!' Kat pulled me in and made me proud to be a woman, one who is able to love God with all her strength and mind. Kat's encouraging and enlightening words along with powerful storytelling are a gift. There is a place at the table for every woman, and every woman will benefit from the encouragement and strength offered in these pages. Put it at the top of your reading pile!"

—Kate Merrick
Author of *Here, Now* and *And Still She Laughs*

"Twenty years ago, I sat down to teach Kat and found myself being taught. Who was this young woman with such a conspicuous love for the Lord, hunger for truth, and abundance of humor and wit? Today when I sat down to read Kat's *No More Holding Back* I had the same experience—I found myself being taught. I was inspired to redouble my efforts to encourage women to pursue theological education in colleges, seminaries, grad schools, and beyond. I plan to share this book widely in the hope that it will encourage others to love the Lord with all their minds without holding back."

—Joseph R. Dodson
Associate professor of New Testament, Denver Seminary

"I wish I'd had this book by Kat Armstrong when I was starting off in ministry, but I am grateful I have it now. I am even more grateful we have a generation of women who will come to understand the truth about God's plan to use women to influence the world through important resources such as *No More Holding Back*. Kat's love for the Word and astute groundedness marks every page of this gem. I'm honored to back this girlfriend and this message with every amen I have."

—Lisa Whittle
Bible teacher, author, and host of *Jesus Over Everything* podcast

"Kat Armstrong had me at the title! *No More Holding Back* is exactly the message that women need to hear. Anchored in the Great Commandment, Kat gives us a framework for loving and leading with all of who God has created us to be—heart, soul, mind, and strength. This book will both challenge and inspire you."

—Jenni Catron
Leadership coach, author, and founder of The 4Sight Group

"For more than twenty years, I've worked alongside women regardless of location, education, or station in life, and there's been a common thread: women hold back. In her book, *No More Holding Back*, Kat beautifully tackles why and then challenges us to consider Jesus's Great Commandment. Loving God with all our hearts, minds, souls, and strength demands we pull up to the table with everything we've got. After reading this book you will never read the Great Commandment the same again."

—Rev. Dr. Jackie Roese
Pastor at large, preacher, author
Founder and president of The Marcella Project

"Kat Armstrong, in her book *No More Holding Back*, has beautifully and clearly reminded the church community how the historical, theological, and ecclesiastical weakening of the role of women in the leadership ministry of the church has not only robbed the church of the natural and God-given gifts, talents, wisdom, and prophetic intuitions of godly women but has also affected the church's response to issues affecting our families, communities, and nations. . . . I recommend this book to those who want to see their communities of faith mature in the knowledge of and in the service to our king."

—Dr. Celestin Musekura
President and founder of African Leadership
and Reconciliation Ministries

"*No More Holding Back* is a book of encouragement to run with the good news of Jesus Christ. It's a book chock-full of God-ordained, *yes-women-can* opportunities. Kat Armstrong pulls the dignity of women made in the image of God from the pages of the Scriptures. Her work is rooted in scholarship and yet so easy to read and apply. . . . *No More Holding Back* reminds us all of what is true: the Lord saves us, gifts us, and commissions us—all of us."

—Sharifa Stevens
Content director for IF:Gathering
Contributor to *Vindicating the Vixens*

"With boldness and wit, Kat wrote the book I needed. As a young Christian woman, I find myself constantly wondering where my place is in my workplace, ministry, and call to discipleship. Kat's book points you to truth and Scripture, and leaves you finding boldness in your identity as a woman of God. . . . Kat left me feeling equipped to embrace my femininity, but she also helped me find strength in my calling from God."

—Grace Valentine
Author of *Am I Enough?*, blogger, and podcast host

NO MORE HOLDING BACK

Emboldening
Women to Move
Past Barriers,
See Their Worth,
and Serve God
Everywhere

Kat Armstrong

W PUBLISHING GROUP

AN IMPRINT OF THOMAS NELSON

Published in Nashville, Tennessee, by W Publishing, an imprint of Thomas Nelson.

Author is represented by The Christopher Ferebee Agency, www.christopherferebee.com.

Thomas Nelson titles may be purchased in bulk for educational, business, fund-raising, or sales promotional use. For information, please e-mail SpecialMarkets@ThomasNelson.com.

Scripture quotations marked HCSB are taken from the Holman Christian Standard Bible®. Copyright © 1999, 2000, 2002, 2003, 2009 by Holman Bible Publishers. Used by permission. HCSB® is a federally registered trademark of Holman Bible Publishers.

Scripture quotations marked CSB are taken from the Christian Standard Bible®. Copyright © 2017 by Holman Bible Publishers. Used by permission. Christian Standard Bible® and CSB® are federally registered trademarks of Holman Bible Publishers.

Scripture quotations marked GNT are from the Good News Translation in Today's English Version—Second Edition. Copyright 1992 by American Bible Society. Used by permission.

Scripture quotations marked THE MESSAGE are from *The Message*. Copyright © 1993, 2002, 2018 by Eugene H. Peterson. Used by permission of NavPress. All rights reserved. Represented by Tyndale House Publishers, Inc.

Scripture quotations marked NASB are from New American Standard Bible®. Copyright © 1960, 1962, 1963, 1968, 1971, 1972, 1973, 1975, 1977, 1995 by The Lockman Foundation. Used by permission. (www.Lockman.org)

Scripture quotations marked NCV are from the New Century Version®. Copyright © 2005 by Thomas Nelson. Used by permission. All rights reserved.

Scripture quotations marked NET are from the NET Bible®. Copyright © 1996–2006 by Biblical Studies Press, LLC. http://netbible.com. All rights reserved.

Scripture quotations marked NIV are from the Holy Bible, New International Version®, NIV®. Copyright © 1973, 1978, 1984, 2011 by Biblica, Inc.® Used by permission of Zondervan. All rights reserved worldwide. www.Zondervan.com. The "NIV" and "New International Version" are trademarks registered in the United States Patent and Trademark Office by Biblica, Inc.™

Scripture quotations marked NLT are from the Holy Bible, New Living Translation. Copyright © 1996, 2004, 2015 by Tyndale House Foundation. Used by permission of Tyndale House Publishers, Inc., Carol Stream, Illinois 60188. All rights reserved.

Any Internet addresses, phone numbers, or company or product information printed in this book are offered as a resource and are not intended in any way to be or to imply an endorsement by Thomas Nelson, nor does Thomas Nelson vouch for the existence, content, or services of these sites, phone numbers, companies, or products beyond the life of this book.

ISBN 978-0-7852-2348-1 (eBook)
ISBN 978-0-7852-2346-7 (TP)

Library of Congress Cataloging-in-Publication Data

Library of Congress Control Number: 2018915211

Printed in the United States of America

19 20 21 22 23   LSC   10 9 8 7 6 5 4 3 2 1

To my husband, Aaron,
I love our blessed alliance. I love us. Thank you
for telling me to go for it . . . about everything.

CONTENTS

Why Are You Even Here?   xiii

PART ONE: THE MESSAGES HOLDING WOMEN BACK

ONE: Women Can't Be Trusted to Learn and Lead   3
TWO: I Don't Have a Lot to Offer   17
THREE: My Greatest Joy Is Marriage and Highest Calling
       Is Motherhood   31
FOUR: I Am Too Much to Handle   47
FIVE: Leading Ladies Don't Fit in Supporting Roles   61

PART TWO: THE CALL TO LOVE GOD

SIX: All Your Heart: Developing a Heart for God   81
SEVEN: All Your Soul: Praising God When Life Gets Real   95
EIGHT: All Your Mind: Staying Open to New Ideas   109
NINE: All Your Strength: Slaying the Forces of Darkness   127

CONTENTS

PART THREE: THE CALL TO SHARE GOD'S LOVE

TEN: Pouring Love Out   143

ELEVEN: Letting Love In   157

Where Do You Go from Here?   169

Acknowledgments   181

Notes   187

About the Author   193

WHY ARE YOU EVEN HERE?

Just stop!"

The conversation in my class at Dallas Theological Seminary came to a shocking halt. The professor had been leading a discussion on women learning about Jesus. Not women *teaching* about Jesus, which some find controversial, but women *learning* about Christ. I had been quick to join the lively discussion because, after all, that's why I was there—to learn. And if women in seminary classes can't engage in a conversation about women in seminary, then where can we talk about it?

Raising my hand, I confessed to the professor, "I'm scared to learn too much about Jesus because I am a woman."

Even as the words came out of my mouth, I'd started to process how ridiculous it must sound to hear a human—an image bearer of God—say that she feared loving Jesus too much. Jesus's Great Commandment, found in Mark 12:30, should compel *all* his followers, regardless of gender, to love him with all of our hearts, souls, minds, and strength, right?

That's when one of my male classmates had started shouting at me: "Just stop!"

He wasn't speaking to the professor or engaging in the class discussion. Instead, his whole body faced me, and he extended his arm, pointed his finger, and raised his voice to warn me: As a woman, I *could* learn too much about Jesus. In fact, when women learn too much about Jesus, he said, they become dangerous; a threat to the local church and a threat to marriage.

You could've heard a pin drop as we waited to see what the prof would say in response.

He slid his glasses off, leaned into his podium, and looked me square in the eye. Choking back tears, he thundered, "*Don't* stop. Don't *ever* stop. Keep going, sister of the faith."

The tension in the room was palpable until the professor called for an unplanned break. Bolting as fast as possible to the women's restroom, I rushed to hide my ugly-cry. Now, in addition to being scared, I was humiliated.

Would you believe that student followed me to the women's restroom? He took one step inside and put a hand on the door to pry it open.

"I have one question for you," he said. "Why are you even here?"

He didn't speak with frustration or anger but with disgust. My desire to learn more about the Bible *offended* him.

With tears rolling down my face and stutter-filled conviction, I tried to communicate that I was a theology student for the same reasons he was, to learn about Jesus. Unsatisfied with my answer, he turned around to leave. It took me several minutes to compose myself, wipe off the mascara smears, and return to class visibly shaken. Nevertheless, I returned.

To be clear, my encounter with this seminary student stood

out as an exception to my overall experience at Dallas Theological Seminary. All my life I've received the gracious encouragement of godly men urging me to pursue God more. I daresay, I know what it's like to have my brothers in Christ in my corner. They are cosigning on the spiritual gifts of women because they want to see everyone thrive. They remind me often that God designed Adam and Eve to co-rule together, co-subdue together, to be fruitful and multiply *together*.

You would think all this support from my brothers would silence any other voices tempting me to approach discipleship judiciously, but it doesn't. Those annoying, sometimes hateful critics like the older gentleman in my class seem to use a megaphone in our lives, able to drown out a whole cheering section. Has anyone told you to ease up, slow down, or stop because you are a woman? If so, I hope I am not the first to tell you that person was wrong.

The progress we've made to dignify women as image bearers of God is not enough. We may be breaking barriers and glass ceilings in the workplace, our communities of faith are finally starting to hear our voices, and institutional change continues across the board. But some people still caution women to stay in their places. Some women like me still wrestle with the tension of Jesus's aspirational words in the Great Commandment and the harsh filter of reality. What would it look like to take a seat at the table without any mental space reserved for uncertainty?

The seminary student's words held power over me for some time. They served as fuel to a fire already burning in my belief system. But he didn't light the match. My nagging concerns were already smoldering by the time I arrived on campus. I worried that my wholehearted devotion to Jesus was a risk and that my

WHY ARE YOU EVEN HERE?

education could potentially upset the powers that be. He served to confirm my suspicions and authenticate my doubts by voicing an all too common viewpoint: some aspects of our spiritual formation are delegated to the guys only.

Somewhere along the way, the church has participated in gendering the Great Commandment. And I'm so over it. We have made loving God with our hearts and souls women's work and loving God with our minds and strength men's work. But the Bible tells a different story altogether: women matter to God as much as men do.

The Great Commandment of Mark 12:30—along with verse 31, which extols us to love our neighbors as ourselves—teaches that God expects the faithful to be all in for Jesus. Nowhere in this passage do we find a reference to male or female. Yet I have been unconsciously reading gender into it as long as I can remember. God did not design half of his priorities for women and the other half for men. Jesus included both genders when he explained that the highest goal of all Christ-followers would be to give completely of oneself to God and then to others. Jesus has a more complete vision for us than we have for ourselves.

I shudder to think that women are shrinking back, diminishing their voices, and resisting the prompting of the Holy Spirit because we feel too uneasy to be all in with our faith. And I'm convinced that even in spaces where leadership does champion women, many of us still allow seeds of doubt to hold us back from serving God in the home, at work, and everywhere in between.

So let me ask you, Why are you here? Have you identified your life's goal? Does the Great Commandment pop into your brain when you have to give an account of your identity and calling? It takes different shapes based on how God has wired you, but at your core, you are supposed to love God with reckless abandon.

Are you tempering your enthusiasm for God or resisting something he has called you to? Should you be raising your hand more at school, work, or church? I've been there. Women are rising into levels of leadership and influence only dreamed of by our grandmothers, but many of us still ask the question, Is it okay for me to do this? Christian women add another layer of insecurity as we wonder if God affirms our advancement. What will our faith leaders think of our progress? How do the doors opening to women align with Christianity? Maybe doubt-filled questions about what we can and can't do occupy our minds because we are not prepared to answer the real question: Why did God put me here?

The Truth Will Set You Free

If the Great Commandment is gender inclusive, then why would we struggle moving forward in every way possible to obey it? Perhaps it's because we've internalized a number of messages about our nature and calling as women that stand in the way of following Jesus with our whole beings. In part 1, I'll share how five such messages have held me back; then I'll debunk them so they no longer hold power over you.

For one, I expected women to be easily deceived, like Eve. A gross misunderstanding of 1 Timothy 2, which reminds us of Eve's role and the sin in the Garden, led to my fear that women are cursed. If I am Eve's daughter, am I even trustworthy with the gospel message or the C-suite at work? I thought I was destined to follow in her footsteps—fumbling obedience. Such foolishness. Believing women are destined for epic failure is so messed up. Turns out the easiest way to get rid of a risk factor is not to bench or restrict women; rather, it is to consider the Savior on the cross, the empty tomb, and the Holy Spirit anointing his people. Curses (real or imagined) die because Jesus lives.

Second, I generally feel like I have little to offer God, even though he asks us to give him our all. I immediately negotiate away prospects of stepping into something new with excuses. When I gain more education, more experience, more confidence—and feel less stressed—I'll really get serious about it, whatever *it* may be. But I know from experience that seasons without hardship don't exist. The always relevant Word of God shows us that sometimes the best we can give Jesus is a broken heart, a troubled soul, a confused mind, and a weakened strength. Because in God's economy, even our smallest offerings have significant value. We may not have a lot to offer, but we must learn the sacred practice of offering everything.

I stumbled most significantly in my faith journey, however, in believing that marriage would be my greatest joy in life, and that motherhood would be my highest calling. When I elevated marriage and motherhood above the first and second greatest commandments, I committed idolatry. For the record, our life stages, ages, relationship statuses, titles, or roles do not determine how we experience the fullness of God's plan for our lives. Dethroning the idols of Christian matrimony and parenthood does not in any way devalue the institution of marriage or the dignity of mothers. But we do need to check ourselves and the words we use to describe things like joy, calling, and purpose for women. Our words matter. They shape our beliefs, which then determine our behavior. Marriage and motherhood will remain valuable, God-given assignments worthy of honor even after we burn up the idols, because all of God's daughters can bring him glory. But wives and mothers do not corner the market on the truest forms of biblical womanhood. Loving God and loving others are life's pinnacles, and we should be sure to say that clearly so there is no confusion.

I also had to admit that I believed I could not be submissive *and* strong. If women are designed for submission in life and in the home, it seemed logical that they could not also be strong. But the two qualities are not mutually exclusive, because *submissive* does not mean *passive* or *weak*. We need to take our cues from Jesus, who submitted to God's will to die on a cross and did so without compromising his supernatural power.

Lastly, I struggled to understand that leading ladies can fit in supporting roles. Everything around me seemed to accentuate the power struggle described in the Fall all those years ago in the Garden of Eden. I felt inner conflict about how my leadership skills fit into subservient roles. I had to reckon with the role of Christ in the church and my life because we are all *his* servants, after all.

My quest to embrace Jesus's calling on our lives meant naming and course correcting these mixed messages. No matter how deeply misunderstanding is buried, the Scriptures can unearth our theological weeds by removing the lies that get in the way of surrender. Pursuing God's most important instructions starts with weed pulling, yanking them out at the root level. Then, free from distractions, we can figure out what Jesus really meant when he cast his vision for women in the Great Commandment.

Researching *heart*, *soul*, *mind*, and *strength* in the Bible, I discovered that the meaning of each word goes much deeper than I anticipated. I can't wait to share my findings with you in part 2. While I assumed *heart* was limited to emotions, *soul* meant spirituality, *mind* equaled brainpower, and *strength* was more natural than supernatural, the Scriptures reoriented my opinions and changed my life forever. In addition to clearing the soil of my heart, the Holy Spirit planted gospel truth through each word study.

By connecting love for God with love for ourselves and others, it's clear Jesus is teaching us that surrender and obedience are connected to our flourishing and are blessings to everyone around us. Part 3 explores how letting love in and pouring love out are the natural by-products of internal change. The fruits of our labor are radical self-love and sacrificial care for the people around us.

I've shared my "just stop" story many times, and the typical response is "Oh no, he did not!" Sometimes, women jokingly ask me to hold their earrings as if they are ready to defend my honor, and almost everyone wants to know his name. Thankfully, I don't know his name. And *he* is not the point.

If I could go back in time with my wits about me, I would have explained to my brother in Christ that women who love God with their all do not endanger the local church or the institution of marriage.

Women who love God with all their hearts, souls, minds, and strength are a threat to egos.

Women who love God with all their hearts, souls, minds, and strength are a threat to power structures.

And women who love God with all their hearts, souls, minds, and strength are a threat to our enemy!

Now I can see God's gracious hand redeeming that fork-in-the-road moment. Because the student asked me a question that I would have to answer the rest of my life. When asked in love, it is a valid question we all need to answer. Although he intended to harm me with the words, "Why are you even here?" God has used them for my good. And I hope he is going to do the same for you.

Through ancient words inspired thousands of years ago, our Savior continues to invite women into his timeless priorities, and in doing so he shows us his plan. Throwing caution to the wind, let's be all in for Jesus. That's what he's always intended for us. No more holding back.

PART ONE

THE MESSAGES
HOLDING
WOMEN BACK

ONE

WOMEN CAN'T BE TRUSTED TO LEARN AND LEAD

But I am afraid that, as the serpent deceived Eve by his craftiness, your minds will be led astray from the simplicity and purity of devotion to Christ.

—2 CORINTHIANS 11:3 NASB

I used to skip church youth group in high school but not to make out with my boyfriend or swipe doughnuts. I was sneaking out so I could slip into Beth Moore's adult Sunday school class at Houston's First Baptist Church.

Even though I didn't know my Sunday school teacher's influence was growing beyond the walls of our church, I wanted to sit under her teaching. Word on the street was, this very Southern lady with very Southern hair would teach the Bible line by line and her class handouts were filled front and back with dreamy fill-in-the-blanks and footnotes. I started attending alongside a few hundred adults as a brand-new Christian eager to learn more about God. By the time I left for college, the class had grown to almost seven hundred people.

One day after class, I asked Beth what I should read next since I had devoured everything she had suggested in class, and she encouraged me to attend seminary. I had never heard that word before, so Beth explained the concept: graduate school for the Bible. My first question about it was telling. Could women go to seminary? She assured me that of course they could, and that was that. I was going.

I rushed through my back door and huddled up with my parents to report the exciting news. Somehow, at some point, I was going to grad school to study the Bible. Get hyped, y'all!

Shocked and flustered, my dad asked me if girls were allowed to attend those places, and he pointed out my undergraduate degree in accounting must come first.

You see, underneath my newfound passion for studying the Scriptures lurked an unconscious belief—for my parents and myself: women learning about Jesus was unusual, and seminary was no place for ladies. But why? Why was my first question about Bible school, "Can women attend?" And what is it about the concept of female theology students that did not sit right with my dad?

Easily Deceived?

Two chapters into God's Genesis story of redemption, we find Eve, the first woman, hoodwinked by the serpent. She doesn't exactly portray us as trustworthy. Since my childhood, I've noticed every storybook picture of the fall of mankind placed Eve in the center of the narrative as the one who was easily deceived. Her failures follow her to the New Testament, when Paul used the sin in the Garden to explain why first-century women in Ephesus were not permitted to teach men. Here's what Paul had to say about it: "I do not allow a woman to teach or to have authority over a man; instead, she is to remain quiet. For Adam was formed first, then Eve. And Adam was not deceived, but the woman was deceived and transgressed" (1 Tim. 2:12–14 csb).

Children's storybook illustrations and the apostle Paul's references paint a bleak picture of womanhood as it relates to following God's instructions. Generations of respected church leaders and theologians influenced by misogyny made it even harder for me to see past Eve's foolishness and resist taking it on as my own.

Marg Mowczko, a brilliant student of the Scriptures, compiled the following list of misogynistic quotes of early church fathers.[1]

The renowned "Father of Latin Christianity," Tertullian, wrote:

And do you not know that you are (each) an Eve? The sentence of God on this sex of yours lives in this age: the guilt must of necessity live too. You are the devil's gateway: you are the unsealer of that (forbidden) tree: you are the first deserter of the divine law: you are she who persuaded him whom the devil was not valiant enough to attack. You destroyed so easily God's image, man.[2]

Thomas Aquinas, doctor of the Church, in the thirteenth century, wrote:

As regards the individual nature, woman is defective and mis-begotten, for the active force in the male seed tends to the production of a perfect likeness in the masculine sex; while the production of woman comes from a defect in the active force or from some material indisposition, or even from some external influence.[3]

Martin Luther, a German priest, theologian, and Protestant reformer, wrote:

For woman seems to be a creature somewhat different from man, in that she has dissimilar members, a varied form and a mind weaker than man. Although Eve was a most excellent and beautiful creature, like unto Adam in reference to the image of God, that is with respect to righteousness, wisdom and salvation, yet she was a woman. For as the sun is more glorious than the moon, though the moon is a most glorious body, so woman, though she was a most beautiful work of God, yet she did not equal the glory of the male creature.[4]

Augustine thought women's only purpose was to help in childbearing.[5] And now, in more recent years, pastor and best-selling author John Piper admits that, historically speaking, women have usually been understood as "more gullible or deceivable than men and therefore less fit for the doctrinal oversight of the church. This may be true."[6]

Famous megachurch pastor Mark Driscoll was instrumental in cofounding several influential evangelical organizations, including the Resurgence, Acts 29 Network, and the Gospel

Coalition. Although his Mars Hill Church has now disbanded, his booklet on church leadership concerning women in ministry emphasizes the widely held belief about women being daughters of Eve based on Paul's words in 1 Timothy 2:

> Without blushing, Paul is simply stating that when it comes to leading in the church, women are unfit because they are more gullible and easier to deceive than men. While many irate women have disagreed with his assessment through the years, it does appear from this that such women who fail to trust his instruction and follow his teaching are much like their mother Eve and are well-intended but ill-informed.[7]

If the writings of influential Christian leaders and theologians throughout history have taught that women struggle to overcome being duped, one might assume it's not wise for women to be students of theology or hold positions of leadership in the workforce or in the church. Based on their interpretations, Eve did not steward her knowledge well, and look where it got us. According to them, it seems the gospel message was not safe with Eve. So that natural next question is, Will it be with us?

Get an entire gender uneasy about loving God with all our hearts, souls, minds, and strength, and you will see how our enemy effectively sidelines women. Women are often told we need to be careful with knowledge, as if a universal holy reverence for the words of God is not for *all* people. I wonder if we are picturing ourselves in a garden, facing a serpent, tempted to be snared like Eve, and disregarding what Jesus redeemed on the cross.

Epic Eden Redo

In light of these misguided and defeating interpretations of Scripture, we may need to remind ourselves that while there are a select few verses that are confusing about the role of women in the Fall and in the church, there are plenty of timeless truths that all agree apply to women: We are image bearers of the one true living God, and we reflect his glory because we were made in his likeness (Gen. 1:26). We were designed to wage war against spiritual forces, to push back the powers of darkness (Eph. 6:10–17). We have been sealed with the Spirit of the almighty God. As a result, we are competent ministers of the gospel (2 Cor. 3:6). We have been called by God into a holy calling, not according to our gender, abilities, or education, but based on God's grace, an irrevocable calling to be God's own (2 Tim. 1:9). Matthew tells us we are the light of the world (Matt. 5:14–16). Sister, Paul says we have everything we need for life and godliness (2 Pet. 1:3), every spiritual blessing in Christ (Eph. 1:3).

And we probably need to be reminded that Jesus's life, death, and resurrection secured us all an epic Eden redo. John, the beloved disciple, started his gospel with "In the beginning" the same way Genesis does. As a parallel work to Genesis, John's gospel is like a second Genesis or a second beginning. By the time we get to John 20 and Christ's resurrection, John has prepared us to see Jesus's words and actions as a movement of redemption. He wrote:

> On the first day of the week Mary Magdalene came to the tomb early, while it was still dark. She saw that the stone had been removed from the tomb. So she ran to Simon Peter and

to the other disciple, the one Jesus loved, and said to them, "They have taken the Lord out of the tomb, and we don't know where they have put Him!" (John 20:1–2 HCSB)

As Peter and John sprinted to the garden tomb to verify Mary's story, they found the stone rolled away and Jesus's linens just as she described. Likely distraught by the missing body, both men headed back to the Upper Room to mourn, but Mary stayed at the grave site to cry. Two angels appeared to Mary and asked her why she was sobbing, but they already knew why. Jesus's body had disappeared, and she didn't know where to find it. Turning around, she saw Jesus, mistaking him for the owner of the garden. Mary supposed Jesus was the gardener and—I want us to catch this—she was not right, but she wasn't wrong either. Jesus *is* the Cosmic Gardener, and he was about to replant humanity in the second garden.

Saying her name, Jesus caught Mary's attention, and she found her Great Teacher. "'Don't cling to Me,' Jesus told her, 'for I have not yet ascended to the Father. But go to My brothers and tell them that I am ascending to My Father and your Father—to My God and your God.' Mary Magdalene went and announced to the disciples, 'I have seen the Lord!' And she told them what He had said to her" (John 20:17–18 HCSB).

For anyone like me, assuming a woman's passion for service is restrained by Eve's example, look again at John's gospel, which highlights Mary Magdalene as a model disciple in the resurrection story.

In the first garden, Eve was placed inside it by God's initiative, and we can assume it was during the day because the lights had already been turned on (Gen. 1). In Mary's story, she comes from outside the garden by her own initiative, and it is still dark outside.

In the first garden, Eve was created *after* Adam, but in Mary's story, she is the *first* person to see the resurrected Jesus—before Peter, before John. She's the first. Hashtag it, please.

In the first garden, Eve faced the fruit-producing tree of life and initiated with her rebellion a curse of death for all. And the fruit was available when she reached for it. In the second garden, Mary Magdalene faced a tomb of death, only to find Jesus had initiated the resurrection life for all. And in the grave, there was no body.

In the first garden, the serpent approached Eve with cunning questions that sowed doubt. In the second garden, angels greeted Mary Magdalene and then Jesus himself appeared, all asking compassionate questions that sowed hope.

In the first garden, Eve hid her naked shame from God's presence before being ousted from Eden. In the second garden, Mary wept without shame in Jesus's presence, and it was Jesus's clothes that were missing.

Eve was deceived, but Mary was commissioned.

Eve rebelled, but Mary obeyed.

The contrast, the repurposing, is so vivid, so clear. I can barely make it through either passage without weeping. I am no longer a gullible daughter of Eve, and neither are you. When my concerns about biblical deception arise within me, I stand condemned as I hear my enemy say, "You are just like your mother, Eve." Instead, I should replay my Savior's words to Mary: "Go and tell your brothers." The curse of being easily deceived died when Jesus rose from the dead.

Somebody get my Wonder Woman crown; I'm feeling inspired.

Run Like a Girl

I wonder what Mary looked like, running with the gospel news to the Upper Room. I know she wasn't rockin' her Nike Frees; she was wearing dusty sandals. I know she wasn't sporting her lululemon Wunder Unders with four-way wicking stretch fabric. She had to scoop up many yards of cloth in her arms to sprint. And what kind of undergarments support the undignified movements of a first-century woman running? I know she was not wearing antiperspirant or a no-pull hair tie for her waist-long hair. So she must have arrived at the Upper Room crusty, dusty, dirty, sweaty, stinky, hair-all-a-mess, out of breath, and maybe with tears still staining her face. What a sight.

In her contribution to *Vindicating the Vixens*, theologian Karla Zazueta reminded me that since Mary Magdalene had been cured of seven demons, likely suffering severely with various mental and physical disabilities before Jesus healed her, she had a reputation for being unhinged.[8] Let that encourage us! Even if our running is undignified and we look crazy for doing it, we still go when Jesus asks us to.

Luke tells us that Mary's words to the disciples in the Upper Room seemed like nonsense to them (Luke 24:11), and they did not believe her. I totally get that. If I had been present to hear Mary out of breath, maybe still crying and speaking with urgency while knocking on that door, I would be looking to Dr. Luke for a medical diagnosis on the formerly demon-possessed lady. Could this be a weird relapse, Dr. Luke? *Don't open the door, people! Whatever you do, do not open the door!* Believing women, trusting their testimony, continues to be an issue for us today.

We should open doors, metaphorically speaking, to our sisters. We should believe women.

Although her brothers in the Upper Room did not believe her testimony (Mark 16:11), Mary Magdalene raised her voice for truth. Let her example be a good reminder to us. Even if our brothers or sisters do not believe us, we still go. We tell the truth: he is risen!

What joy it must have brought Christ to redeem her physical and mental handicaps, knowing her future would include moving with speed to communicate the most important message the world has ever heard. Our past does not define our future.

Now, I don't run unless I am being chased, but I've been told by runners that it provides a great space to think. So I wonder what Mary was thinking while she was running. I imagine her processing, *I was destined to carry this message. I was healed to take this message. I was delivered to deliver this message.*

In 2014, Always produced a Super Bowl commercial called "Run Like a Girl" that currently has more than sixty-six million views on YouTube.[9] To promote their feminine products and win the "epic battle" of young girls' confidence, they filmed responses to the prompt, "Show me what it looks like to run like a girl, fight like a girl, throw like a girl." True to life, the adults (and boys) shown at the beginning of the ad pretended to run, fight, and throw with subpar skills. Per the actors' role-playing, doing something the way a girl does looks stupid, vapid, weak, and silly.

By contrast, the director asked *young* girls what it means to run like a girl, and without hesitation one child declared it means to "run as fast as you can." The point of the three-minute ad is this: somewhere along the way, doing something "like a girl" has become a put-down. It is used to humiliate people when it should describe excellence. And I think we do that in Christianity too. Before it became a modern-day criticism, "You run like a girl" could have been an ancient compliment in Jesus's day for women like Mary Magdalene.

Free to Run

The same year I admitted to my classmates that I was afraid to learn too much about Jesus, Father Juan Solana began construction on a retreat center in Galilee. He wanted to build a respite for Holy Land tourists. Under Father Juan's leadership, construction workers in Israel unexpectedly uncovered the ancient ruins of Magdala (the town where Mary Magdalene would have been raised). The discovery of the Magdala stone[10]—the oldest carved stone block depicting the second temple—and a first-century synagogue was an archaeological marvel. As I was digging up the theological weeds of gender bias and the role Eve had played in my life, people were excavating Mary Magdalene's hometown to uncover something lost.

In 2017 a friend offered to sponsor me on a trip to the Holy Land with a tour called "Women in the Word," led by Dr. Jackie Roese. Morning Star Tours was offering their first female-only trip to Israel to study women of the Bible, and I was on it. Two days before leaving, Dr. Roese reached out to me to see if I would preach about Mary Magdalene on-site in Magdala. She pointed out I would be preaching in a place where Jesus's feet walked the earth. My text back was, "Yaaassss! Thank you! Thank you!"

As Israel and the city of Jerusalem prepared for its seventieth Independence Day celebrations, I was preparing a message about my freedom in Christ. Although I rarely cry-talk, I broke down in front of the crowd of women gathered at Magdala to study Mary Magdalene's life and see the ancient ruins of her town. Struggling even to breathe, let alone speak, I tried to retell my "just stop" story. Repeating my professor's words to our small band of women, I implored, "Don't stop. Don't *ever* stop. Keep going, sisters of the faith."

After my sermon I used my GoPro to film the diggers sifting through rubble at the Magdala excavation site, and I realized that the gifts of women are much like the ruins being unearthed right in front of me. Our gifts and talents, buried for centuries, have always been present, but now we see that elevating women's voices aligns with the Scriptures. Nothing about our gender hinders us from studying the Scriptures, seeking to know God better, or sharing those truths with others. Nothing about our gender should keep us from following God's lead in our homes, with our families, or in the workplace. Like Mary Magdalene, we need to go with the gospel into our spheres of influence at a pace so urgent: We. Must. Run. Run like a girl. Because Jesus commissions us to and because he is risen indeed.

Mary does more than just represent that the testimony of a woman can be trusted, that God chooses women for kingdom purposes, and that we, too, can be used by God to go and tell our brothers (and sisters) his good news. Mary Magdalene is Eve's literary redemption. If Jesus is the second Adam, raised from dust by the power of the Spirit, then Mary Magdalene is the second Eve. Obeying Jesus, Mary fulfilled her mission and was worthy of the truth entrusted to her. The gospel is safe with women.

Nothing will rival her message. Jesus is the news. But we might unleash a generation of women if we teach them that secondary to the message of "Jesus is risen" is this: a woman was the first preacher to literally *bring it*.

I wish I had been introduced to Mary Magdalene's no-holding-back heroics before the term *seminary* entered my vernacular. Maybe my first question to Beth Moore would have been "How fast can we run there?" rather than "Can girls go to seminary?" Instead of questioning what races we should enter, what pace we should keep, or what distance is appropriate for our gender, you and I must believe that we are not gullible daughters of Eve but rather commissioned daughters of the King. Sister Mary Magdalene left us a heroine's legacy.

Let's follow in her footsteps.

Discussion Questions

- What have you been taught about Eve as it relates to all women?
- Is that message implied or specific in your church?
- What about Mary Magdalene's story stands out most to you?
- Metaphorically speaking, what gifts are you uncovering about yourself?
- If Mary Magdalene is the first preacher to literally bring the gospel message, how should that influence our communities of faith?
- How would you describe your faith-life right now? (sitting, standing, walking, running, limping)
- In what area of life you do need one of God's epic redos?

TWO

I DON'T HAVE A LOT TO OFFER

For they all gave out of their wealth. But she, out of her poverty, put in what she had to live on, everything she had.

—MARK 12:44 NET

Because I am afraid of heights, I almost missed a once-in-a-lifetime chance to see Masada, the ancient fortress built by Herod the Great, while traveling through Israel. The stronghold, which towers over the Judaean desert and overlooks the Dead Sea, fell at the end of the First Jewish-Roman War, when Roman troops scaled the cliff to kill the Sicarii rebels seeking refuge on the mountaintop. The battle ended when the Roman garrison found 960 men, women, and children who had ended their lives by mass suicide.

Holy Land tourists flock to the famous site to walk through Herod's palaces and review history, and climbers and adventure seekers hike up the Snake Path to the fortress for fun. Since swinging hundreds of feet above the ground on a cable throws me into a panic, I didn't want to ride the thirteen-hundred-foot-high gondola to enjoy the plateau views, and no one who knows me well could imagine me hiking up Masada, especially not for kicks. So our tour group and I devised a plan that would enable me to enjoy the site from the ground while the rest of the ladies journeyed upward.

But on the bus ride to Masada, our tour guide casually mentioned that all Israeli soldiers are sworn in on Masada after completing their basic training. Naturally, I started to picture Wonder Woman climbing the Snake Path. Wonder Woman is my superhero of choice, in part because the newest movies in the franchise have an Israeli actress, Gal Gadot, playing the princess of the Amazon warriors fighting for justice.

Thinking through the implications of Ronnie's words, I realized Gal, an Israeli soldier before becoming an actor, would have been commissioned at Masada. Wonder Woman climbed Masada! Throwing my safety plan out the window, I spontaneously decided I would ascend on foot like Wonder Woman's alter ego, Diana Prince, while the rest of the group rode to the top.

Ten thousand steps later and an hour longer than expected, this city-loving girl raised her crossed forearms, the way Gal does in the movies, and posed for a picture at the top of Masada. Dripping in sweat and red-faced from the trek, I have an Instagram post to commemorate my victory.[1]

Before leaving the great rock, I moseyed through the air-conditioned gift shop to amass proof of my accomplishment, picking out two souvenir shirts. Shirt one says, I CLIMBED MASADA. Subtle. Shirt two says, MASADA WILL NOT FALL AGAIN. Truth.

While shopping for my cotton memorabilia, I stumbled upon

jewelry made with tiny coins set in precious metals. Official enclosed papers indicated that each coin resembled the widow's mite mentioned in Mark 12:41–44.

As the gift-shop salesperson attempted to gain my purchase of a $500 widow's-mite ring, I started to see the irony of spending a lot of money on something that represented the smallest of offerings in the New Testament. I laughed off her enticements by saying I didn't have a lot to offer. She said, "Try me."

Although I did not end up buying a ring that day, our negotiations inspired a hard conversation with God. I realized that, instead of choosing each day to present my entire life to God, I usually end up telling him I don't have a lot to offer. Based on Jesus's teachings of the widow's mite that occurred immediately following the greatest commandment, I think he, too, responds to our negotiations with, "Try me."

Give What You Have

We've already seen how the Word of God has dismantled gendered assumptions about the call to love God wholly, and it has subverted any fears about being daughters of Eve. It has also elevated the Great Commandment beyond our capacity to fulfill it, a daunting prospect. Living up to Jesus's most essential instructions can be as scary to me as climbing a mountain or riding a gondola up a thousand feet in the sky.

When a scribe approached Jesus in the temple courts to ask which command is the most important of all, Jesus moved the conversation from the temple courts into the court for women, where the priests set up offering receptacles.[2] The same audience listening to the greatest commandments were now following Christ into a different part of the temple so he could give a teaching illustration.

Watching many people contribute to the offering, Jesus called his listeners' attention to a poor widow giving out of her poverty: "Then he sat down opposite the offering box, and watched the crowd putting coins into it. Many rich people were throwing in large amounts. And a poor widow came and put in two small copper coins, worth less than a penny" (Mark 12:41–42 NET).

As the least valuable person in her world, the widow donated her mite in a mighty act of surrender. Her culture overlooked her as a member of the lowest class of society and the most vulnerable gender, insignificant to anyone of importance and lacking the financial means to make a difference. But Jesus zoomed in on her gift as an example of doing his will:

> He called his disciples and said to them, "I tell you the truth, this poor widow has put more into the offering box than all the others. For they all gave out of their wealth. But she, out of her poverty, put in what she had to live on, everything she had." (vv. 43–44 NET)

Noted theologian J. R. Edwards added valuable commentary to the scene:

> In purely financial terms, the value of her offering is negligible—and unworthy of compare to the sums of the wealthy donors. But in the divine exchange rate things look differently. That which made no difference in the books of the temple is immortalized in the Book of Life. How powerfully

ironic is the word "more" in Mark's description. Everything about this woman has been described in terms of less, particularly in comparison to the scribes and wealthy crowd. And yet, the contrast between her genuine piety and faith and the pretense of the wealthy is beyond compare.[3]

Maybe you are in a life season of abundant blessings, comfort, joy, and prosperity. Glory to God! He is the giver of all good gifts. Savor these treasures. Anticipate more days like this in your future. Or maybe you are grieved, anxious, confused, your body is failing you, and you want to give up. Theoretically, many of us know that we don't need to clean up before we meet with God, enjoy his presence, or experience his favor. But in practice, I like to wait until I'm in a "good place" to give back, serve my community, or take a risk.

No sooner do we set the bar higher for our great priorities of loving God and loving others than we second-guess our ability to fulfill them. Out of fear that we bring too little to the table, we reveal through our lack of confidence that our value system is much different from God's. He values the small, treasures the insignificant, elevates the humble, and counts a widow's mite as worthy. As our priorities shift, our value system must too. In our world of all or nothing, Jesus teaches us "all" does not equate to "a lot."

According to J. R. Edwards, "The chief purpose of the widow is as a model of discipleship. No gift, whether of money, time, or talent, is too insignificant to give if it is given to God."[4] Giving of ourselves when we have little to offer, when it's all we've got, is worthy of God's commendation—even when it seems our economy deems it the least valuable gift. Every gift counts, especially those that come from hard-up places.

Serving God, really sticking with him through thick and thin, will at times mean loving him with a broken heart, troubled soul, confused mind, and weakened strength. And that is okay, more than okay. Such sacrificial service has eternal significance.

Broken Hearts Count

Pastor Tiffany and I go back to a time when the hardest part of life was studying for exams. Multiple people on campus suggested we meet because they knew (before we did) that we would be besties. Promotion after promotion, Tiffany rose through several leadership roles on a church staff to land in the pastor to women position at a megachurch in our area. She leads with authenticity and vulnerability, which has made her journey through trauma all the more harrowing.

When we threw Tiffany's baby shower, we knew her son David would need intensive cardiac care after he was born, but no one knew his life on earth would span less than two months or that all of his days here would be a fight for survival. After David passed away, all I could think about was my dearest friends having to close the door of their nursery both physically and metaphorically.

While she grieves the loss of her son, she continues to minister to the women of her church. It looks different post-tragedy, and it is not without pain, but she shows up to love her people. She can do so with greater insight into their grief and with more skill to listen with compassion, but she is nothing less than faithful to pour herself out when she feels empty. Tiffany's heart is broken, and she is a pastor. She can be both at the same time because Jesus motions his students to watch a trifling widow give a small contribution—and make a huge impact.

Scott Sauls, a writer and pastor, says it best: "Sometimes the best, most life-giving way to lead is by suffering well. Sometimes the best, most life-giving way to lead is by refusing to allow death, mourning, crying, or pain to dictate the story line of our lives and of history."[5]

How will we respond when Jesus invites the brokenhearted, disillusioned, distracted, and limping women of our generation to his table? Will we pass on our seats because we do not feel up to it? To all the women nursing broken hearts, serving on empty does not equate with failure. Our Savior experienced heartache too. He knows our pain. He sees our suffering. And he joins us there. Instead of viewing our place in his presence as a staff member reporting our progress, maybe we should remember that we will find a kind Savior giving us our turn to mourn in his arms. "He heals the brokenhearted and binds up their wounds" (Ps. 147:3 HCSB).

Troubled Souls Count

Each young woman applying for leadership in Polished (the nonprofit outreach ministry I cofounded ten years ago) must tell us about her faith journey and how she would share the good news of Jesus with a coworker if the opportunity presented itself. We include a statement on the application assuring women that everyone who has ever answered the question feels inadequate to do so, and those uneasy feelings do not come from God. Apply anyway.

One applicant honestly admitted that she was not sure she believed that Jesus was her Savior anymore, but she hoped that by staying connected to our group and spending time with women who are convinced he's theirs, she might reclaim some of her faith. No sooner had I finished reading her story than I reached out to treat her to lunch. Pouring jalapeño ranch onto our street tacos, we started talking about what prompted her to apply and the reservations she felt about church. She courageously shared that her soul was "troubled," and she was caught off guard when tears started rolling down *my* cheeks. I knew exactly what she meant. Doubts creep into my life, too, leaving me wondering if any of this Jesus stuff is real. There is something to be said about people like us approaching God for healing. Jesus says, "Come to Me, all of you who are weary and burdened, and I will give you rest" (Matt. 11:28 HCSB).

If we limit who can serve Jesus to only those Christians who have no doubts, we would have no one giving back. Sometimes in church we get worked up and concerned about our siblings in Christ who are struggling with doubts, but I would have to agree with author Anne Lamott, who wrote, "The opposite of faith is not doubt, but certainty."[6] It would be healthy for us to accept our friends' asking hard questions and searching for answers, because their pursuit is an expression of faith.

To all you wavering women still choosing to flip the pages of this book, keep at it. Beyond our world's praises for giving a slice of our excess time, money, and talents to God is a Savior cheering for the have-nots ready to give him everything. Maybe instead of having it all together, we bring our disillusioned selves to Jesus with confidence in his heaven-oriented value system.

Thomas, the doubting disciple of Jesus, gets me. We both need to see to believe. Reacting to the news of Jesus's resurrection, Thomas said, "Unless I see the wounds from the nails in his hands, and put my finger into the wounds from the nails, and put my hand into his side, I will never believe it!" (John 20:25 NET). Eight days later, the disciples, Thomas included, were shocked when Jesus appeared to them to say, "Peace be with you!" (v. 26 NET). Looking into the doubter's eyes, Jesus asked the cynic to examine his scarred body, and Thomas's disbelief vanished.

For the women who won't get the privilege of seeing Jesus's marks, we can witness one another's healed scars. You and I are now the body of Christ. The apostle Paul put it this way: "Now you are Christ's body, and each of you is a member of it" (1 Cor. 12:27 NET). I'm not suggesting we replace Jesus with humans, that our scars replace Christ's, or that we make ourselves God. But I do recommend we take 1 Corinthians 12:27 seriously.

What if we showed up for the people questioning the ways of God by revealing our scars? No platitudes, empty words, or feeble attempts to fix. What if people around us need our presence and vulnerability more than our canned answers? In the absence of an embodied Christ, could our outstretched arms, marked by hardships, relieve troubled souls of doubt?

If you fight a tendency to mistrust, keep calm and carry on. Suspicion of church leaders, confusion on Christian doctrine, or skepticism about Christians reveals a search for authenticity, consistency, and relevance. Seeking God with reluctance still means seeking God. Keep your eyes on Jesus, the Author and Perfector of our faith, and lean in to the body of Christ too.

Confused Minds Count

"My faith is on pause right now," she told me. Twenty-five years old and on her first job at a large firm, a young lady confided in me after I said at a conference that Christianity was confusing. In full agreement, I consoled her and mentioned that I, too, find my faith frustrating at times. She asked me how I could justify feeling disoriented and still keep the faith.

Opening up my Bible to Philippians 3, I told her I keep reaching forward. The apostle Paul wanted to know Christ, and he faced serious setbacks in his journey. He said the key is forgetting what is behind and reaching toward what is ahead of us (Phil. 3:13). Paul wrote, "Not that I have already reached the goal or am already fully mature, but I make every effort to take hold of it because I also have been taken hold of by Christ Jesus" (Phil. 3:12 HCSB).

If we wait to sort out all of our Bible questions or solve the problem of evil before we unpause our relationship with God, we could be waiting a long time. However counterintuitive, suspending faith goals to figure out life is a waste of time. If you feel perplexed about a passage of Scripture, annoyed by one of the stories of the Bible, flustered by the injustice we see in the Scriptures, or disenchanted by our spiritual leaders—you are human, and real life doesn't always make sense immediately. Press on and reach forward.

The supernatural experience of knowing Jesus can at times seem unsettling. I think that's why Paul used the word *mystery* in most of his New Testament letters, a total of eighteen times. You can find *mystery* in Romans, 1 Corinthians, Ephesians, Colossians, 2 Thessalonians, and 1 Timothy. Describing

Christianity, Paul wrote, "The mystery of godliness is great: He was manifested in the flesh, vindicated in the Spirit, seen by angels, preached among the nations, believed on in the world, taken up in glory" (1 Tim. 3:16 HCSB). If the greatest church planter of all time and the author of half of the books in the New Testament gave us permission to hold in tension the enigma of a knowable God, we should take him up on it.

Weakened Strength Counts

Most of this book was written from hospitals while my mom, the strongest person I know, was battling a chronic bone infection in her right ankle. On New Year's Day 2018, my husband and I were crawling into bed after a lazy holiday when my phone started to ring. My mom was concerned about the growing bump on her leg that now seemed more like a tumor ready to explode.

Although the cancer screen came back clear, the infection had burrowed deep into her anklebone, and they needed to remove half of the bone to save it. That meant months in rehab without the ability to drive, walk, or take care of herself, followed by another surgery putting in a concrete substance to fill in the missing parts, and many more weeks of physical therapy.

When she asked me to bring her laptop from her home office up to the long-term care facility unit, I tried to argue some sense into her. In my opinion, she needed to rest, not work. But my feisty Latina mama firmly corrected me by saying she may not have physical strength, but she could still contribute to her team in a meaningful way, and there was no way she was going to lie in bed watching TV all day. Raising my hands in surrender, I promised to have Aaron set up a make-shift office. Suit yourself.

My mom struggled with the depression we all face when our bodies fail us, but she took God at his word, that God's grace is sufficient for us, for his power is perfected in our weakness (2 Cor. 12:9). Lacking control over her recovery and the self-sufficiency to take care of herself, she opted to listen to her doctors, follow the health plan of her social workers, and continue to work in her weakened state.

While I usually conserve my energy for a time when I can really make a difference, my mom's experience gave me a visual for choosing to love God with weakened strength. If Paul was right— "When I am weak, then I am strong" (2 Cor. 12:10 HCSB)—I need a paradigm shift.

More than Enough

My friend Beth was willing to hang back with me at the base of Masada while the rest of our tour group rode the gondola, but when I decided to climb like Gal Gadot, she said she would come with me on my adventure. Little did I know, Beth is a former army captain who served at Fort Riley with the First Infantry Division as a military intelligence officer. And now she serves as a pastor at her church, sharing her gifts of leadership and preaching with her congregation and using her position of influence to fight for social justice. She's basically a real-life Wonder Woman. Over the course of our hike, I needed to borrow from her example of strength and faith several times over because there's no way I would have made it to the top without Beth leading the way. None.

Halfway up the Masada Snake Path, Beth mentioned she doesn't have a thyroid due to cancer. Say what? She explained on one of our breaks that she's on Synthroid, a thyroid medication that can create a sensitivity to heat—this, while we were hunched over the railing with the sun scorching our backs. We have plenty of video footage of us doubled over in pain, panting heavily, and poking fun at ourselves as more experienced climbers rushed past us at record speed. Our captions all involved some variation of "We. Are. Dying."

I failed to bring water with me for the ascent, a rookie move, for sure. But Beth saved the day. She graciously offered to share what little water she had packed to ensure we both got up the mountain. She kept turning around to hand me the water bottle, assuring me there was enough. It struck me sometime later that Beth's sacrificial generosity put flesh on the lesson God was trying to teach me about giving what we've got even if we are operating at a deficit.

Pitted against our intentions to follow God, we face a very real enemy looking to kill, steal, and destroy us. His lying tactics aim for our confidence. He tells us we are not enough, and we don't have enough, and this is not the right time. He whispers we need to clean up, shape up, gear up, and get more of something before we can serve. He turns his nose up at our failings and recommends sitting this season out because of the legitimate constraints on our schedules, bank accounts, or emotional strength.

Satan makes valid points to hold us back, to dissuade us from giving from our wealth of knowledge, abilities, or income. But Jesus runs his kingdom with the currency of love. Our world obsesses with surplus while Jesus cheers for those of us giving from our emotional and financial poverty. We may not have a lot to offer, but we can give him everything we've got. To the broken-hearted, troubled, confused, and frail, Jesus says, "Try me."

With him you have more than enough.

Discussion Questions

- What would it look like to love God with a broken heart?
- What would it look like to love God with a troubled soul?
- What would it look like to love God with a confused mind?
- What would it look like to love God with weakened strength?
- What would it look like to offer the little you have to God?

THREE

MY GREATEST JOY IS MARRIAGE AND HIGHEST CALLING IS MOTHERHOOD

> You must not have any other gods besides me. You must not make for yourself an image of anything in heaven above, on earth below, or in the waters beneath. You must not worship or serve them, for I, the LORD your God, am a jealous God.
>
> —DEUTERONOMY 5:7–9 NET

Meh."

Back in history, when text messaging did not exist, and people liked—dare I say, *preferred*—to talk on the phone, I had a milestone conversation with Kelly, a friend from back in my college days. I was inviting her to one of my small-group Bible studies, but she responded with, "Meh." Don't you love when people keep it real? Although I did not pry, she explained that she was having a hard time connecting with God because she was single, childless, and wishful for her life to be different.

It sounded foreign to me, a twenty-three-year-old newlywed. What was the disconnect?

For nearly an hour, I listened while she cried through the difficulties of attending church as a single. Her problem wasn't with any specific congregation or even the one she was currently visiting—it was bigger than that. It was the conservative evangelical church as a whole. Describing her painful season of life, she revealed messaging from Christians that added salt to her wounds, from church announcements that assumed everyone who attended was a married parent to the seemingly unending questions from loved ones about when she would "settle down." Even the phrase "settle down" implied she was wandering aimlessly, floating above real life, or lacking stability.

She was describing how this messaging came through sermons—both implied and specifically—when pastors would apply the text to men in their jobs and to women in their roles of caregiving as mothers or wives. She gently suggested that this subliminal teaching had been building over time and was now coming out consistently: Christian women should be married and have children. No wonder many singles feel lonely and disenfranchised from the local church.

She explained that it was excruciating to feel as though the very roles eluding her—those of wife and mother—were the positions that Christianity promised would make her a fulfilled woman of God. It felt as if the *only* litmus test for female godliness came from pastors quoting the "submission" passage:

> In the same way, older women are to be reverent in behavior, not slanderers, not addicted to much wine. They are to teach what is good, so they may encourage the young

> women to love their husbands and to love their children, to
> be self-controlled, pure, homemakers, kind, and submissive
> to their husbands, so that God's message will not be slan-
> dered. (Titus 2:3–5 HCSB)

At this point in Kelly's life, studying the Bible felt futile because she didn't know how to apply Scripture to her life. She felt out of place, excluded, and undervalued.

From my viewpoint, Kelly, in her late twenties, had every-thing going for her. This woman was in love with Christ, her character was above reproach, she had a great job, she owned her own home, *and* she was gorgeous. She was a catch. In fact, while she was confiding, I was mentally matchmaking. Keeping my mouth shut and trying to listen, I was distracted by her real problem: timing. I believed it was just a matter of time before she would find Mr. Right. "Just a matter of time" turned out to be one of my most flawed designations for my unmarried friends, because the apostle Paul said it's better to stay unmar-ried (1 Cor. 7:8).

After some reflection, I've come to understand and appreciate Kelly's bravery in seizing this opportunity. She helped me under-stand her reasons when I didn't care as deeply as I do now. She told the truth when it exposed her otherness and my lack of awareness. She was patient in her explanation when I had trouble stepping into her shoes. Moreover, she risked confiding in me, someone who had not yet proved herself safe. Kelly was courageous.

In one unforgettable moment during the conversation, Kelly said she was in a "holding pattern." Thankfully, the Spirit prompted her to use that exact phrase so I could relate, because I struggle with impatience. (My husband, Aaron, says I am the least patient person in the world, which is obviously ridiculous; he doesn't *know* every person in the world.) Kelly's words described what many of us may have experienced when idling on an airport tarmac on the first day of vacation.

I ended my conversation with Kelly by thanking her. Not sure how to process it all, I told her I had strong suspicions that I had internalized and forwarded these lies, too, playing a part in her pain. And for that, I was so sorry. After we hung up, I cried, knowing I was guilty of glorifying marriage and motherhood.

What followed next were countless conversations with women who echoed Kelly's personal experience over the course of several years while my husband served as the singles' minister at our church. As my own awareness around the subject heightened, my ears started to perk up every time Bible teachings and ministry strategies supported the consensus of my sisters.

And then I had to look inward. On my journey to better understand Jesus's greatest commandments, I realized I was making a dangerous swap by replacing marriage and motherhood for heart, soul, mind, and strength in that short but powerful verse Mark 12:30. I paraphrased it as "love the Lord as Aaron's wife and Caleb's mommy." Being Aaron's wife and Caleb's mom makes me happy and adds significance to my life. I fill a purpose in those roles. However valuable and noble I find them, neither is worthy of golden calf status.

Whether intended or not, I believe the conservative evangelical church communicates to women that marriage is our greatest joy and motherhood our highest calling. Kelly was right. And I had been guilty of preserving these dangerous messages because they served me.

Dethroning Idols

Taking valuable things and turning them into false gods is a familiar cycle for God's people. The Israelites waited approximately forty days for Moses to come down from his meeting with God on Mount Sinai. Three months post-rescue, God's people lost sight of his past deliverance and the Promised Land in their future. Scripture says that when they "saw that Moses delayed in coming down from the mountain, they gathered around Aaron and said to him, 'Come, make us a god who will go before us because this Moses, the man who brought us up from the land of Egypt—we don't know what has happened to him!'" (Exod. 32:1 HCSB). Gathering up their precious metals, the impatient Hebrews convinced Aaron, Moses's brother, to reshape the gold and silver into an image of a calf.

It seems far-fetched that in the absence of a spiritual leader's presence I would offer up my beloved Kendra Scott earrings to satisfy my need. But then again, I am accustomed to subconsciously changing the words of popular Bible verses, reshaping them to fit the narrative that marriage and motherhood determine a woman's happiness and our most meaningful contribution to society.

Jesus said, "Go, therefore, and make disciples of all nations, baptizing them in the name of the Father and of the Son and of the Holy Spirit" (Matt. 28:19 HCSB). But I wonder if some of us process those words this way: "Go, therefore, and make disciples before you get married, and baptize in the name of the Father, Son, and Holy Spirit before you start a family." Jesus said he came to give life and give it in abundance (John 10:10), but I think many women feel as though Jesus came to give us married life and kids in abundance. The apostle Paul encouraged Christians to not grow weary in doing good (Gal. 6:9), but I think many of my sisters in Christ have paraphrased that so that it reads, "Do not grow weary; soon you will have a spouse and soon you will have a family." Paul taught Christians that we were created in Christ Jesus for good works (Eph. 2:10), but do we reshape that timeless truth to mean women were created just for a marriage and a family?

Internalizing the Scriptures is partly about the verses we hear in church and the way our leaders interpret and apply them in their teaching, but it's also partly how we process those truths through our lived experiences. The idolization of marriage and motherhood is a result of both. Inaccurate holding-pattern messages from our faith leaders plus majority culture voices are a dangerous combination left unchecked by God's Word.

If we look closely again at Jesus's first and second Great Commandments, we find that in Christ's priorities there is nothing that speaks to a particular role of wife or mother, husband or father, boss or subordinate, young or old. It simply says to love God with our all and share that love with others. If Jesus elevates this commandment above all the others, we should too.

Let's look closely at Matthew 28:19–20, the Great Commission, which says, "Go, therefore, and make disciples of all nations, baptizing them in the name of the Father and of the Son and of the Holy Spirit, teaching them to observe everything I have commanded you. And remember, I am with you always, to the end of the age" (HCSB). We see nothing there that suggests that our life goals should revolve around marriage or parenthood.

We've set up two idols as the be-all and end-all for women:

marriage and motherhood. Is it any wonder that those human-made gods don't live up to the hype even in the best of unions and the most glorious of parenting adventures? In direct opposition to the idolatrous idea that godly women find satisfaction only in matrimony, Jesus is the unmarried embodiment of joy. And the Bible is full of examples of unmarried women and men who are seen, accepted, and purposed by God to work for the common good of all people.

Single Lady Influencers

One such influential single lady was Mary Magdalene, whom we looked at in chapter 1. She held the distinction of being the first person to share the good news of Jesus's resurrection. There is no mention of a husband or children in the narrative. Mary was used by God to herald the gospel, preach to the disciples, and testify to the resurrection of Christ. You might even say she was the apostle to the apostles.

In the Old Testament, Miriam, Moses's sister, was held in high regard. She led the women of Israel in song and dance to celebrate and worship God for delivering them from the Egyptians after crossing the Red Sea. Many years after she rescued her baby brother, Moses, from the Nile River, God used Miriam's singing voice to lead the congregation in corporate worship (Exod. 15:20–21). She was even titled a prophetess (also in verse 20), and by Paul's standards, the gift of prophecy ranked as one of the most influential and desirable of the spiritual gifts (1 Cor. 12:28). Though Miriam was not married and had no children, she played a key role in our faith history.

These unmarried women, along with many others, were central to the work of their faith communities, and their voices were heard. In today's churches, however, many singles don't feel they have a place.

Feeling Fulfilled in All Life Stages

During my husband's time as a singles' minister, I often had to console the ladies in his group who felt that they had yet to achieve the Christian ideal for their lives. They remarked that they didn't know how long they could "wait on God" for their "life to begin." They were eager to "get to the next phase of life" and "graduate from the singles' ministry."

Most of the conversations included tears: tears of anger concerning God's timing, tears of frustration because they felt they had all this "potential" to be a fantastic wife and mother but no opportunity to activate those passions, tears of confusion because they felt they were circling the tarmac of God's will. Many were convinced, entirely sure, that after they had a family, all their dissatisfaction with work and life would be alleviated. If they could just get there. Preparing their whole lives for the ultimate joy of marriage, they were ready to get on with it.

Bestselling author and speaker Carolyn Custis James seems to have lived through many of these conversations, too, because in her book *When Life and Beliefs Collide*, she described the mindset so well:

> Single women with this point of view are waiting for the plan to commence. Until a husband arrives on the scene, they are

on hold or must default to a second-class plan that is not nearly as good or meaningful as that of a married woman. Singleness is perceived by many in the church (including some singles) as a woman's private purgatory—a suspended state of uncertain duration useful only as a bridge to marriage.[1]

The belief system fueling the disappointment of the women in our singles' ministry reached a fever pitch when one young woman asked me to pray God would "hurry up and bring her husband to her so that her life of purpose could begin." Wait. What? Her choice of phrasing packs a punch. Joy Beth Smith, author of *Party of One: Truth, Longing, and the Subtle Art of Singleness*, addresses this head-on:

> Singleness is not simply a season to be weathered, a waiting room, or a holding cell. It's not temporal by design, and it doesn't exist only to usher you into something greater. Singleness is a valid life stage, one in which you can experience as much joy, spiritual growth, and fulfillment as any married person.[2]

Context makes these stories all the more unsettling. All the women mentioned above approached me because we attended a church that firmly believes in catalyzing women. Time and time again they proved they cared about us, all of us, and they put their money where their mouths were by hiring and elevating women into leadership positions, supporting a vibrant ministry to singles, and consistently making sure singles were included in church-wide initiatives. It wasn't a passive value of the church. Elevating women with dignity in all life stages was at the core of this organization, and it showed in their women's teaching team and the representation on their leadership teams.

How is it that young women attending *that* kind of church, one that overtly supports them, could still be affected by the belief that marriage would be the pinnacle of delight? The ideology was much more pervasive in Christian culture than one church could defeat. We must overpower these holding-pattern messages with the truth so that women, alongside men, can live up to Jesus's priorities at every age and stage.

Ironically, I probably hear from at least one married woman per week who wants to admit that, while marriage and parenthood are beautiful and wonderful, they still haven't found what they are looking for. Do you know any unhappily married women? Any women who do not enjoy parenthood the way they envisioned? Yep. Me too.

This holding-pattern issue Kelly described in our phone call does not affect only the single ladies. Conservative evangelical church culture trains Christ-followers to believe that life will matter most when we get to the next step in life. For singles, that means marriage. If you are married, that means kids. And then, and only then, will you realize your potential and fulfillment. This line of thinking, in my opinion, is one of the most effective tools for Satan to distract Christ-followers from loving God with all their hearts, souls, minds, and strength . . . right now. Especially women.

Our Highest Calling: Loving God and Others

Married for ten years before becoming a mom, I used to park near the children's entrance to church because of convenience.

Big mistake. After being asked in that hall routinely when I was going to start having kids, I finally wised up and chose another church entrance. My childless presence contrasted the sea of adults juggling car seats and tiny humans, which prompted innocent questions about my uterus's business. Since Aaron's Sunday morning responsibilities as a pastor prevented him from arriving with me, I was often greeted by churchgoers and asked if I had heard of our singles' group before they noticed the ring on my finger. It felt as if showing up to church without a counterpart or without kiddos was reason for pity. If I wasn't being asked about finding that special someone, I faced questions about when I was going to have kids. It was exhausting and demoralizing.

Before Caleb was born, I made the mistake of admitting to a devoted Christian grandmother that I lacked the maternal inclinations I thought mothers should have and that I was hesitant to start a family. She thought this was close to heresy. While looking at pictures of her grandchildren, she asked *when* I would be starting a family of my own. Although infertility is a battle I have never fought, it pains me to think about the wounds these kinds of conversations perpetuate for women struggling with infertility.

After I explained the various reasons I didn't feel ready for kids, she said emphatically, "You are missing out on the highest calling God has on your life." Her words pierced me and stunned my confidence. Flinching inside, I wondered if it showed. She was well-intentioned but wrong. Being a mom is a high calling but not the highest. That's reserved for God only.

Her comments made me question my identity and doubt myself. *Was* I missing out on the highest calling of my life? What if I never wanted to have children? What if I wanted to have kids but would experience infertility? Is parenthood the zenith? Jesus did not have children; was his lifestyle not enough?

While I processed my confusion, Aaron reminded me there's nothing in the Great Commandment that excludes people from living up to their fullest potential if they don't have kids or never get married.

Dethroning the idols of Christian marriage and motherhood does not in any way devalue the institution of marriage or family. It elevates God to his unrivaled throne. That means we must change family-centric churches into Christ-centric churches. Which will require an adjustment, for sure.

Becoming Christ-Centric Churches

In order to make changes, we first need to change our language in hopes our values will follow suit. Rejecting phrases like "Not until I was married did I really understand what Christ had done for his church," "Marriage is the greatest joy of my life," and "Marriage is the best picture of how Jesus loves his church" would be a good start. All of those resemble the truth enough to create confusion. Our single sisters can understand what Christ has done for the church without getting married. And marriage is a picture, just one, of how Jesus loves his church. But as a single Christian author, Joy Beth Smith would propose, "Joy is not spelled M-A-R-R-I-A-G-E."[3] Innocent hyperboles from majority culture can have severe consequences for the women in our churches deciphering their value.

For the record, being married can bring great joy. I sure like it. But it is not the greatest joy of my life or yours—that joy is reserved for God alone. I wonder what would change in our faith communities if we really took to heart the apostle Paul's opinion that it is better to remain single (1 Cor. 7:8 NET). In my perfect world, I imagine a church that simultaneously and confidently affirms parents, spouses, *and* singles as indispensable to the mission of God.

While we're at it, let's abandon the notion that "you can't understand the love of the Father until you become a parent," or that "parenthood is the best discipleship method," or that "my kids are my life." The ability to comprehend the love of the Father comes from the Holy Spirit. It is not something we inherit with children. Jesus excelled at making disciples without biological or adoptive children of his own. There is no limit to what God can do in and through single women, women struggling with infertility, or women who choose never to have a family.

From my friend Elizabeth's point of view, as a single woman and former singles' pastor, married men, who control much of the conversation about singleness from the pulpit, usually promote womanhood for singles as an extended period of marriage preparation. She told me, "Simply put, the church tends to not have a place for single women because they don't have what gives them value in Christianity—a husband and children. Women are valued for what they do for other people, namely, kids and a husband, not for who God has made them to be and what gifts they can uniquely contribute to the body."

We could also take account of the single and/or childless women in our lives. By now the Spirit may have already brought names and faces to your mind—women so dear, so invested in your lives, you can't imagine life in Christ without their presence. In my own life it's JoAnn, Michelle, Lisa, Sue, Jana, and Dawn.

Seek your people out; remind them that the body of Christ is not complete without them in it. Look them in the eye and remind them that they matter.

And then we can reckon with the important questions: Are the childless esteemed in our neighborhoods, in our spheres of influence, in our small groups and organizations? Do we value their contributions to the world as we do those of missional mothers or devoted wives? And if not, how can we be agents of change among the people we influence?

If we need to pull people aside at work or at church and lovingly ask them to reconsider the way they phrase things, let's do it. If we need to make space for our sisters in rooms and situations usually devoid of their inclusion, let's do it. If we rarely get the opportunity to hear their voices, let's amplify them. Because this is what the kingdom looks like.

You Are Mission Critical

Six years after our "holding pattern" conversation, Kelly married the godly man of her dreams. Sadly, their honeymoon phase came to an abrupt ending when they faced an extended season of infertility. As the doctors pronounced part of her anatomy a "failure," she felt like one all over. A family was the end goal, after all. Intimately acquainted with feelings of isolation, loneliness, and depression, Kelly followed a familiar pattern in her faith: she felt shame.

Unlike during her journey as a single, Kelly now felt resentment toward God in addition to her shame. If Kelly were writing this, she would tell you she felt as though she "did her time as a single" and should be rewarded for her faithfulness. She'd also be the first to tell you these thoughts don't align with the Bible and she had some internal work to do, but also that the mixed messages women receive in church and from Bible teachers contributed to her discontent.

She can remember the first time that the concept of motherhood was equated to a more direct connection to God for her. It was during a sorority chapter meeting in which a guest speaker testified that there was no female experience that would bring someone as close to God as giving birth naturally. I happened to be present for that talk too. I can remember it clearly.

After college Kelly was overwhelmed with an onslaught of questions from well-intentioned church members encouraging her to "hurry up" before she was too old, because her children might be born with mental or physical disabilities. But nothing compared to the comments about her catching up with her younger brother, who was "beating her in the race" to have kids. Let's not cause our women without children to feel they must always play catch-up in Christianity.

Thankfully, Kelly chose to immerse herself in the Word of God, specifically studying the women of the Bible. God's promise is sure: the truth did set her free (John 8:32). She read commentary after commentary about women like Hagar who gave God a name: "The God Who Sees" (Gen. 16:13). And she felt the conviction of the Holy Spirit as she absorbed the Scriptures. The God who sees pain was Kelly's God, and she started to own that.

Kelly and I are going to celebrate twenty years of friendship right around the same time this book is published. And it's not lost on me that without Kelly there might not be a book to publish. Her story and those of the countless other brave women willing to share their experiences with me have brought to light the way we hold our sisters back from obeying and enjoying the Great Commandment. They are the reason I wanted to write this message.

If we could accomplish anything together while your eyes are on these pages, I pray that all women, and I really do mean *all*, will feel appreciated, recognized, and showered with encouragement because King Jesus loves you. No life stage, age, or role determines your value, worth, or ability to love God and love others. Additionally, we need you. The body of Christ needs devoted spouses, mission-minded parents, *and* godly singles.

As my dear friend Nika Spaulding would say, you are mission critical.

Discussion Questions

- What about Kelly's story connects to your own story?
- Have you heard the message that marriage and motherhood are the greatest joys of godly womanhood? If so, where do you hear those messages?
- How has that message influenced you?
- Who could you encourage this week who may have experienced this message?
- How would our communities of faith change if we embraced all ages, stages, and roles as assignments from God?

FOUR

I AM TOO MUCH TO HANDLE

> Now Deborah, a prophetess, wife of Lappidoth,
> was leading Israel at that time.
>
> —JUDGES 4:4 NET

A young woman approached me after a speaking engagement to confide that she had been accepted into a seminary in the fall. Full scholarship. As you can imagine, I was overjoyed and let it show. Picture me giddy, making happy claps while bouncing. She hadn't even graduated college, but she had caught the attention of the academics at her potential future grad school. And she was convinced at this point in life that serving God as a professor was her next assignment as a Christ-follower. Academics were literally calling. I thought this conversation was headed for hugs and happy tears. I thought she was going to ask me about any tips on navigating seminary as a woman, and I thought maybe, just maybe, we could nerd out together on some upcoming theology book releases. Sadly, she followed up her good news with a noticeable countenance of fear and distress.

Evidently, she had trusted her mixed-gender small group with this same news. A college-aged young man from her group explained that she should be "careful" about this decision—that the more a woman learns about the Scriptures, the less attractive she becomes to godly suitors because godly men want to lead their wives spiritually.

He applauded her desire to know God more, study the Scriptures, and fulfill her calling, but he said, "The stronger a wife is, the harder it is to be her spiritual leader." I was shocked. This statement is not only untrue; it contradicts everything in Jesus's summary of godly living that we've read in the Great Commandment.

This young woman wanted to know more about Jesus *and* wanted to get married eventually. And she was expressing something I hear often: if a single woman truly invests her all into her relationship with Christ, she lessens her chances of finding a godly husband. Which should she prioritize? Besides being shocked by her questions, I was dismayed by the young men in her life dissuading her pursuit of God, and I was trying to find words to help her navigate the situation.

She went on to explain that when a single man becomes godlier, he is *more* desirable in Christian circles. When a single woman becomes godlier, she becomes *less* desirable because she is then more difficult to lead. She was trying to figure out how to move forward into her calling but not get ahead of her future husband in the meantime. Before I could give her a hug and pray over her, she tearfully explained she felt like she was "too much to handle." The enemy's tactics are so sly. If we're not struggling with feelings of inadequacy, he goes at us from the other extreme and convinces us we are too good at loving God with our all.

These young men were basing much of their advice on a very small but loud minority group within the evangelical community that believes marriage brings a spiritual authority demotion for women based on the passage that says, "Wives, submit to your husbands as to the Lord" (Eph. 5:22 NET). But they fail to mention that in the original language there is no verb *submit* in that verse. You would have to borrow the word *submit* from the previous verse to understand that Paul was talking about mutual submission for both husband and wife. Verse 21 says, "Submitting to one another out of reverence for Christ."

It seems many single women are caught in a terrifying lose-lose scenario. If they can overcome the idolization of marriage and motherhood so prevalent in many churches and embrace every season of their lives as an opportunity to run hard after God, their commitment could jeopardize finding a godly husband. And there it is: Satan's checkmate. He's busy keeping us focused on certain roles or threatening us with the futility of our devotion to God. Neither will do.

There is a big difference between what we know and what we believe. We probably *know* that godliness is always a good thing for all people at all times, but I wonder if we *believe* it. I think the stories I am going to share with you prove that many people believe the godlier a woman becomes, the harder she is to date, and that strong women are hard to lead. The thing is, *strong* leaders do not struggle to submit; *bad* leaders do. Submission is not hard for *strong* women (or men); it's hard for *prideful* women (and men).

Willing Submission

My bestie Sarah remembers considering turning down the esteemed young singles' class directorship at her church because the joke going around called it the "kiss of death." In her circles, leadership skills were a liability for eligible godly women. As a female class director, your image would change overnight into someone who was undatable because you were now deemed too spiritual. They wanted single ladies to be godly, but not too godly. Sigh. We fare no better in the workforce, according to the chief operating officer of Facebook, Sheryl Sandberg. She said, "When a woman is successful, people of both genders like her less."[1]

Living close to a university means I have the privilege and joy of getting to know some college-aged women who love Jesus. Lots of our conversations revolve around dating, and my marriage remains a constant source of curiosity. They want to know how we make it work.

As I treated a college sophomore to a cup of coffee, she traced her dating history with her current boyfriend to catch me up to speed. He wanted to know for sure if she would submit to him if they get married. They had been dating for all of three weeks, and he wanted to know how she sees her role in marriage and if she will let him lead her. She could not have been twenty years old, but he was planning on their next date to discuss pretty major life decisions, like grad school locations and how to manage her money. Excuse me? According to him, submitting to his leadership now, before they became exclusive, was good practice for the future. Picture me choking on my banana loaf to cough up the words: Gross. No.

Free dating advice: If the prospect wants to talk about your submissiveness to his leadership, get the heck out of there, because I am afraid for you. Uber home, phone a friend, and break up with him. Nowhere in the Scriptures do we see a prescription for the kind of male leadership that controls, manages, or forces someone to submit. Submission, by definition, is not something asked of us; we offer it willingly as unto the Lord.

Never in my sixteen years of marriage has Aaron, my husband, ever asked, suggested, or ordered me to submit. We can't require people to defer; they do so by choice. I gladly lean on my husband as my closest confidant. When he speaks into my life, I listen. And we haven't crossed a decision yet where we were not willing to wait to be on the same page and move forward in unison.

The last question my college friend had for me that day was related to knowing too much about the Bible. Her boyfriend did not grow up in church, and he admitted he lacked Bible knowledge. One of the most attractive things he liked about her was her faith, but he worried he would have a hard time catching up to her familiarity with the Scriptures. She asked me if she should tell him she was getting into a new Bible study that fall on campus. Would it lessen her chances for the next date?

You are going out with him again?

Hard pass. If Bible knowledge or Bible study attendance is a deterrent to your boyfriend, find a new guy. If loving God with your all is unattractive to him, he's probably not the one for you. If growing in your relationship with Christ prevents the man you are dating from being able to lead you well, the issue is his understanding of leadership.

Too Strong to Follow?

A young woman and friend confided to me in tears that, to her horror, the all-knowing StrengthsFinder test revealed she is . . . wait for it; it's really, *really* bad . . . an activator. Can you hear the scary movie music in the background? She excels at making things happen—she's a mover and a shaker. As a catalyst for change, she was made by God to start ministries and lead people to Jesus like it's her job. Actually, it is her real job. She is one of the best evangelists I know. This young woman is a force against evil. She slays. How is being an activator terrible, you may ask?

In her mind, an activator equals initiative-taker, which equals not passive, which equals not submissive, which equals bad wife, which equals ruined marriage.

Yeah. We went from the StrengthsFinder test results to her nonexistent marriage being ruined by her ministry accomplishments. After digging a lot deeper with a series of questions, I finally wrapped my mind around her logic. Her talents and disciplines that have been used by God to win souls, the same gifts the Spirit had fanned into flame, could undo her marriage. Or so she feared. She wasn't dating anyone. Not engaged. No online dating profiles. But she had already convinced herself that the very things energizing her would be the death of a godly marriage.

I've lost sleep over my activator evangelist friend. This is not how it's supposed to be; that much should be clear. It deeply troubled me that evidence of God at work in her job could be twisted into a danger to her future relationships with men. When we turn faithful integrity into something that will destroy a marriage relationship, we are not thinking correctly.

Another dear friend, Courtney, called to process her date with a guy she'd met at work. After their second date, she had some concerns because he wanted to talk about submission in marriage. I know. This is not second-date conversation material. Then again, maybe it's saving her. But it came up, and he expressed a grave apprehension for my friend's joy in her job. Women who work, he said, concern him. He asked her, "Will you be able to submit to my leadership?" Part of the conversation—or should I say interview—included his suggestions that she should not get too good at her job. Solid work ethic and job satisfaction could lessen her devotion to a future family and would make her more resistant to his leadership. This is ridiculous on so many levels. As a matter of fact, we can see from biblical examples that successful women are to be desired.

Judge Deborah

Serving in judgeship of the nation of Israel, Deborah was a married woman of valor leading the people of God with wisdom and courage (Judges 4). She wasn't just the lone woman to judge Israel; she also held the unique dual function of both fiery judge and authoritative prophet.[2] In a role similar to the reign of a king, she ruled over the military as judge, and she spoke with authority on behalf of God to his people as a prophetess. And she wasn't God's plan B. That much is clear from the text. God considered her an indispensable asset. He chose her to lead.

I wonder what her husband thought about her calling. If he was anything like the Christian men highlighting the talents of their wives today, he likely found great satisfaction knowing his counterpart was glorifying God in the assignment God had given her.

I'm bringing up Deborah's story to point out the fact that she was a strong woman *and* married. And we don't see any indication from Scripture that her success as a leader was against God's plan or getting in the way of a healthy marriage. Deborah wasn't too much to handle in God's eyes, even though she had national influence, even though her people recognized her leadership, and even though she delivered the Word of God to his people with authority. Let's make room in our churches and workplaces for women like Deborah. Because God did.

The Proverbs 31 Woman

Another successful woman was the Proverbs 31 woman. She was considered the epitome of a woman of valor—so much so that King Lemuel's mother advised him to marry someone like this. Let's look at her qualities.

1. This woman would be a hardworking person who "selects wool and flax and works with willing hands" (v. 13 HCSB). Her textile spinning and weaving would be a proof of her skills and work ethic.
2. "She evaluates a field and buys it; she plants a vineyard with her earnings" (v. 16). Her elbow grease and investment capital would create provisions for her household and additional income if she sold the grapes or wine.
3. "She sees that her profits are good, and her lamp never goes out at night. She extends her hands to the spinning

staff, and her hands hold the spindle" (vv. 18–19). She's so industrious that she even has enough to share with the poor (v. 20).

Apparently the Proverbs 31 woman's work did not diminish her ability to be a good wife and mother, or even to be submissive—or the king's mother would not have chosen her.

New Testament Disciples

The New Testament reinforces this idea. Consider the band of women traveling and supporting Jesus's ministry financially as Luke described:

> Soon afterward He was traveling from one town and village to another, preaching and telling the good news of the kingdom of God. The Twelve were with Him, and also some women who had been healed of evil spirits and sicknesses: Mary, called Magdalene (seven demons had come out of her); Joanna the wife of Chuza, Herod's steward; Susanna; and many others who were supporting them from their possessions. (Luke 8:1–3 HCSB)

These women disciples not only followed Jesus, absorbing his teachings, but also offered their funds to support his mission. Examples like these and the Proverbs 31 woman show us that a woman's passion for her work, success on the job, or willingness to follow Jesus is not a negative.

Strong and Spirit-Led

I joined a few friends in a dreamy restaurant to celebrate one of their birthdays. Cheers and cake and girlfriends, yes. We settled in for a laid-back, upbeat evening toasting our mutual friend before a sugar coma. I was seated next to a dynamite professional woman who asked me how my marriage worked. Her winsome smile turned into apprehension as she waited to hear my answer. Knowing a little about our story, she asked me if it bothered Aaron that I was seeing some success in my organization. I said no. She asked me if Aaron disliked how much I enjoy my job. Again I said no. Then she asked me if I thought Aaron was the only man on the planet that appreciated my ambition. I quickly answered, "No, of course not!" With a mouthful of bread, I asked her to help me understand where all these questions were coming from and why the sudden interest in my marital relationship with Aaron.

She explained she was crushing it at work. I thought that should be a win, something we would all celebrate, but to her it felt like a curse. While she was earning promotions at work, she wondered if her male friends at church would see her success as a positive in a future spouse. She worried that her intelligence and business acumen would discourage godly guys from asking her out on dates. I leaned in, as Sheryl Sandberg would like us all to do, and locked eyes with her to say that Aaron's favorite quality of mine is ambition. He is more practiced at saying "Go for it, babe" than I am at taking risks. If God willed for her to marry and wired her for promotions, work responsibilities, and favor in her endeavors, then she could find a man who would appreciate her. I truly believe that, and yet I know her fears are based in real-life experience. Again, Sheryl Sandberg confirms this view of women: "Professional ambition is expected of men but is optional—or worse, sometimes even a negative—for women."[3] The same is true in some sections of the church.

As tears welled up in her eyes, I reminded her, "Your strength and ambition are good." I hope I didn't lie to her. I really hope Christians want women to be strong in the Lord and successful in life in the same way we do for men.

I'm concerned that we use our deficient teachings on submission and leadership as a weapon against strong women. It's a tragedy because deference is a beautiful theme of the Bible; it's modeled within the Godhead, and it's a timeless exhortation to all Christ-followers. I love the way Carolyn Custis James teaches about godly submission:

> The common belief is that biblical submission entails passivity and that therefore a godly wife ought to leave theology to her husband. But such a notion is surely misguided. Christian submission, which finds its ultimate example in Christ, is an act of strength, understanding, and determination. Jesus modeled not a mindless, limp compliance but a thoughtful vigorous resolve. His actions did not result from a power struggle with his father but expressed their union. Jesus was not defeated; he was determined to fulfill his father's will.[4]

Maybe we've overemphasized a woman's submissive role and, in doing so, lost sight of the fact that submission is not the hallmark of a Christian woman's character.

Focus on Fruit

The fruit of the Spirit is the hallmark of a Christian, male or female. Instead of asking if this woman can be led, we should ask, "Is this woman *Spirit*-led?" Instead of asking if she can submit, we should ask, "To *whom* does she submit?" And the answer should be the Spirit. Women can and should be simultaneously mighty and humble because Jesus was.

I began this chapter with the story of a young woman who confided in me after a speaking engagement. She made sure to tell me that a "good catch" for a *woman* would need to be a man pacing ahead of her spiritually, but a good catch for a *man* is someone running just a tad slower or, at most, right alongside him in unison. The young men in her small group suggested she slow down so that a man could catch up. So, she was holding back. This should grieve us.

Put another way, the pace of a godly male leader should not determine the speed of a woman's pursuit of God. Everyone needs to pick up the pace, and women should not hold back out of fear they will alienate a good prospect for a spouse. This is not a drill, people. The front lines need to be filled. For the sake of the gospel, everyone should be running. And according to Paul, we should be running in such a way to win the prize (1 Cor. 9:24).

If, by the power of the Holy Spirit, we focus on loving God with all our hearts, he will shape us into wholehearted women, and that is a good thing. By the same strength that raised Jesus from the dead, disciplining ourselves to love God with all our souls will form us into soulful women, and that is praiseworthy. The sustaining power of God's Spirit, the same that holds the world together, can renew our minds and make us mindful disciples of Jesus, and that is commendable. The force that conquered death lives inside of us now and grows our strength, which is pleasing to God and a blessing to the faithful.

For every woman out there thinking she is too much to handle, maybe she could think this way instead: How can I use what God has given to me to bring him glory and to work for the common good of all people? Instead of obsessing over the line between godly enough to date and too godly to marry, we should reorient ourselves around this passage: "We are His creation, created in Christ Jesus for good works, which God prepared ahead of time so that we should walk in them" (Eph. 2:10 HCSB).

We can't play small. And not because we are a big deal—quite the opposite. We can't play small because God's mission to reconcile all people to himself is too important. You were handcrafted with every single part of your personality, disposition, and wiring for the good works God intended for you to carry out. Don't hold back. You are a part of something bigger than yourself. If that ends up putting off potential suitors, maybe you deserve different ones. If that means your marriage looks different from someone else's in your church, so be it. Jesus is worthy of a lifetime committed to die-hard convictions.

Discussion Questions

- How do submission and strength work together?
- How do you process the word *submission*?

- How can submission and strength coexist in the life of a believer?
- How have you seen submission used to limit women?
- How could we raise the next generation of women both to practice submission and to be strong in the Lord?

LEADING LADIES DON'T FIT IN SUPPORTING ROLES

> She does her work with energy, and her arms are strong. She knows that what she makes is good. Her lamp burns late into the night. She makes thread with her hands and weaves her own cloth. She welcomes the poor and helps the needy.
>
> —PROVERBS 31:17–20 NCV

L anding my first real job postcollege at a consulting firm was a dream come true. Although I found the work pace grueling at times, most of the firm's clients were well-respected Christian nonprofit organizations or Christian leaders, and my job was to train clients on technology that would reach more people with the gospel. To me it didn't matter if I answered phone calls or stapled handouts; the thrill of the job was the bigger picture.

Once, after I had completed a website walk-through with a client, he opened up the conversation to talk about my aspirations at the company. As I gushed over the impact our firm was having and the role I got to play, I could see the client raise an eyebrow. When I finally took a breath from rattling off all the reasons my job was awesome, the client asked me if I was married and if I could see myself continuing to work after my husband got a job as a pastor. The questions seemed out of left field. But yes, at this point in life, the answer was yes. Unassumingly, I flashed a huge smile to deliver my answer.

"Rein it in," he said. "Rein it in, sister. You can't help your husband the way God designed if you keep at it this way." Huh? What way? And what does "this" refer to? Looking to my left and right to see if I was the only one tuned in to this strange turn of events, I returned my gaze back to the client. He scribbled a messy one-sentence note on a Post-it, folded it, and handed it to me while whispering, "Make sure and check the Bible, sweetie." The note said, "Start in Genesis."

Reliving the conversation with my coworkers, one of them suggested the client was probably wary of a pastor's wife with career ambitions. Another implied the client referred to the role of women as helpers to their husbands in general. In any case, I was intrigued and started to reread Genesis as the client had recommended. Although I think his advice did not accomplish what he intended, I'm grateful he suggested I do my homework and that I start in the first book of the Bible. The exercise has done me good.

According to the creation account in Genesis, God created women to be helpers. Like it or not, that's the truth. But not the kind of help an administration assistant gives to the boss, a babysitter provides to an overwhelmed momma, or an African American woman supplied while serving in an oppressive white household, as we see in *The Help*. No. Even leading ladies fit the supporting roles God has designed for us. I promise. The question is, What kind of support does God have in mind for women? 'Cause nobody puts Baby in the corner.

I'll give you a hint: *all* people fit supporting roles, because the Christian life is one long act of service. Hollywood might promote A-list and B-list actors filling a hierarchy of character roles, but in the kingdom of God, Jesus holds the leading role and we are all *his* supporting cast. Far above every ruler and authority, power and dominion, and every title given in our age and every age to come, God put everything under Christ's feet and appointed him as head over everything for the church. Jesus is the One who fills all things in every way (Eph. 1:21–23).

Biblical womanhood's archetype is Eve, the first woman created by God from Adam's rib. Compelled to form Eve, God explained her necessity by saying, "It is not good for the man to be alone" (Gen. 2:18 NIV). His solution was to make a helper "suitable for him" (NIV). What I wanted to know was, What did Adam need help with in Eden, and what does *suitable* mean?

Indebted to Carolyn Custis James, I bring you some of the points she made in her life-changing book *When Life and Beliefs Collide*: Did Adam need a domestic engineer, someone to manage the house? No, he didn't. No houses needed keeping in the Garden of Eden. Did Adam need someone to cook? Nope, they ate from the garden produce. Did he need someone to help with laundry? Again, no. They were naked. What about the kids—did Adam need someone to raise the kids? At this time, they had no children to rear. Did he only need a companion to alleviate his aloneness? Nope. He was in the presence of God, where all fullness of joy can be found (Ps. 16:11).[1]

While Adam did not require assistance with managing a house, cooking, cleaning, doing laundry, raising children, or companionship, all of those essential responsibilities must get done in modern households. In my own family, most of those weekly tasks fall to me. Yet while my contributions to our family are priceless, they do not compose a woman's truest purpose on earth. I would go so far to say that it doesn't matter how the obligations of "adulting" are delegated, as long as they get done.

Helping is not limited to being a wife and a mother. We can maintain that both roles are beautiful expressions of someone who is helpful while recognizing that they are not the definition of a helper.

Adam's placement in the Garden happened before Eve was even fashioned. The sequence of events matters, because it speaks to the purpose of all women and men. Right before God said, "It is not good for the man to be alone; I will make him a helper suitable for him," he charged Adam with cultivating Eden. *That's* what Adam needed help with—he needed a partner to nurture the earth.

God told both Adam and Eve to "be fruitful, multiply, fill the earth, and subdue it. Rule the fish of the sea, the birds of the sky, and every creature that crawls on the earth" (Gen 1:28 HCSB). Could it be that in addition to gendering the Great Commandment, we have done the same with the Cultural Mandate? Have we made *multiplying* women's work and *ruling* men's work? Listen closely, people of the Book: the preeminent role of any woman (and man) is multiplying *and* ruling.

But don't let the word *multiplying* throw you. One might assume that Eve and Adam's responsibility of multiplying is limited to procreation, but the problem with this is Jesus. As the hallmark of the Christian faith, he is preeminent over all creation (Col. 1:15), which means that whatever God appointed Adam and Eve to do, Jesus accomplished the same—flawlessly. Jesus fulfills all of God's tasks and orders, yet he was single with no biological children. So, how did Jesus fulfill the mandate to be fruitful and multiply, to fill the earth? Jesus reproduced disciples. To all the women passing on their faith to their friends, coworkers, family members, children, and loved ones, keep at it. Making disciples is our thing (Matt. 28:19).

I wonder what kind of tidal wave of revival would break out if we took to heart God's words in the Garden. If women are equally created to rule the earth and reproduce Christ-followers alongside men, does that change the way you approach life? Do we assign more value to a woman's calling to multiply than we do to her calling to rule? Do we assign more value to a man's calling to rule than we do to his calling to multiply?

My time spent in Genesis did not confirm that I needed to "rein it in." Instead, it revealed that I had been gendering the Cultural Mandate, and I have a hunch my client was guilty of doing the same thing. That got me to thinking about the word *helper* beyond the book of Genesis and his suggestion to "check the Bible." I needed to know more about this word, whether it showed up other places in Scripture, and how to apply it to my life.

Ezer

Does God make mistakes? I'm not as meek and maternal as I think I am supposed to be. Maybe the God of the universe was napping when I was formed in my mother's womb. These thoughts kept running through my head before Carolyn Custis James's research introduced me to the Hebrew word *ezer* (pronounced "ay-zer"), which is usually translated "helper" in the Old Testament. Oh sister, hold on tight. Tissue after tissue in hand, I worked through her findings to discover this quote that would set me free: "The military language associated with the word *ezer* ties the same bold imagery to the strong helper. She is a valiant warrior conscripted by God, not to fight against the man but to fight at his side as his greatest ally in the war to end all wars."[2]

Wow. I had to see for myself. Pulling out my trusty Bible concordance, I started to systematically look up each of the references to the Hebrew word for "helper" in the Old Testament.

Twenty-One References to *Ezer* in the Old Testament

Ms. James was correct. Of the twenty-one times[3] that *ezer*, the helper, appeared in the Old Testament, it is best translated as "warrior." James wrote in her book *Half the Church*, "Scholars tallied up the twenty-one times *ezer* appears in the Old Testament: twice in Genesis for the woman, three times for nations to whom Israel appealed for military aid, and—here's the kicker—sixteen times for God as Israel's helper."[4] The point is, God was protecting them like a warrior in battle. See for yourself where *ezer* appears (underlined in each verse below).[5]

1. Genesis 2:18 NASB

Then the LORD God said, "It is not good for the man to be alone; I will make him a <u>helper</u> suitable for him."

It's clear that Adam needed Eve's help, but as we've already discussed, the help didn't have anything to do with household duties traditionally assigned to a mom.

2. Genesis 2:20 NASB

The man gave names to all the cattle, and to the birds of the sky, and to every beast of the field, but for Adam there was not found a <u>helper</u> suitable for him.

Unlike the animals Adam was naming, he had no counterpart.

3. Exodus 18:4 NASB

The other was named Eliezer, for *he said,* "The God of my father was my <u>help</u>, and delivered me from the sword of Pharaoh."

Moses envisioned God delivering the Israelites from the sword of Pharaoh when he named his son Eliezer, which means "God is my help." The word *helper* is used in this passage of Scripture to describe God himself; more specifically, God's help secures military victory for the Israelites.

4. Deuteronomy 33:7 NASB

"Hear, O LORD, the voice of Judah,
And bring him to his people.
With his hands he contended for them,
And may You be a <u>help</u> against his adversaries."

As Moses prayed for Judah, he asked God to hear his prayers and be Judah's help against his adversaries, because the tribe of Judah marched as the head of the tribes, the literal front line of every battle. The word *help* here describes God's helping Judah with military success so that his tribe would keep the Israelites safe.

5. Deuteronomy 33:26 *NASB*

> "There is none like the God of Jeshurun,
> Who rides the heavens to your <u>help</u>,
> And through the skies in His majesty."

Moses prayed for Asher while ascribing to God his glory. There is no one like God, Moses said, for he rides the heavens to help us. In no uncertain terms, his prayer was about Asher crushing it in life because of the security God afforded him. The word *help* in this verse references God's divine protection for Asher.

6. Deuteronomy 33:29 *NASB*

> "Blessed are you, O Israel;
> Who is like you, a people saved by the LORD,
> Who is the shield of your <u>help</u>
> And the sword of your majesty!
> So your enemies will cringe before you,
> And you will tread upon their high places."

Moses told all Israel that they would be blessed because the Lord is a shield of protection and sword of majesty. *Help*, again, is God's providing military assistance that results in triumph.

7. Psalm 20:2 *NASB*

> May He send you <u>help</u> from the sanctuary
> And support you from Zion!

The author of this psalm used the word *help* to say, "God's help sustains us."

8. Psalm 33:20 *NASB*

> Our soul waits for the LORD;
> He is our <u>help</u> and our shield.

God is the helper in this verse, and he was helping by shielding his people in battle.

9. Psalm 70:5 *NASB*

> But I am afflicted and needy;
> Hasten to me, O God!
> You are my <u>help</u> and my deliverer;
> O LORD, do not delay.

God was the helper in this verse, and he was helping by delivering his people in battle.

10. Psalm 89:19 *NASB*

> Once You spoke in vision to Your godly ones,
> And said, "I have given <u>help</u> to one who is mighty;
> I have exalted one chosen from the people."

About the warrior King David, *ezer* refers to "God's help to his chosen ruler."

11. Psalm 115:9 *NASB*

> O Israel, trust in the LORD;
> He is their <u>help</u> and their shield.

Unlike the nations worshipping silver and gold idols made by human hands, the Israelites worshipped Yahweh, who was their "help and shield."

12. Psalm 115:10 NASB

> O house of Aaron, trust in the LORD;
> He is their <u>help</u> and their shield.

"Yahweh is our help and shield" became their mantra.

13. Psalm 115:11 NASB

> You who fear the LORD, trust in the LORD;
> He is their <u>help</u> and their shield.

This is the third time in one psalm that God is called the helper of his people, and each time it is in reference to his help as their shield in battle.

14. Psalm 121:1 NASB

> I will lift up my eyes to the mountains;
> From where shall my <u>help</u> come?

This verse should sound familiar to some who might sing a similar song on Sunday morning at church. Singing a processional song of ascent on the annual journey to Jerusalem, God's people sang that the Lord was on their side. Their help came from God himself.

15. Psalm 121:2 NASB

> My <u>help</u> *comes* from the LORD,
> Who made heaven and earth.

This is the second verse in that song of ascent, and later in the same psalm the author said if God was not their helper they would be attacked and swallowed alive, the waters of the Nile engulfing them with raging waters.

16. Psalm 124:8 *NASB*

> Our <u>help</u> is in the name of the LORD,
> Who made heaven and earth.

The thread weaving these hymns together is the word *ezer*, which is used every time to describe God's helping hand in battle. God's people escaped slavery because their help was in the name of Yahweh.

17. Psalm 146:5 *NASB*

> How blessed is he whose <u>help</u> is the God of Jacob,
> Whose hope is in the LORD his God.

This beautiful psalm speaks of God the helper aiding his people by executing justice on their behalf.

18. Isaiah 30:5 *NASB*

> "Everyone will be ashamed because of a people who cannot
>   profit them,
> *Who are* not for <u>help</u> or profit, but for shame and also for
>   reproach."

The use of the word *help* in this verse and the next two are of nations to whom Israel appealed for military aid.

19. Ezekiel 12:14 NASB

"I will scatter to every wind all who are around him, his <u>helpers</u> and all his troops; and I will draw out a sword after them."

God is promising to destroy the prince of Judah and all of his troops, or helpers. Although the word *helper* here is not used to describe God, it is still used in a military context.

20. Daniel 11:34 NASB

"Now when they fall they will be granted a little <u>help</u>, and many will join with them in hypocrisy."

During a time of intense persecution against the Jews, God is declaring he will help deliver them.

21. Hosea 13:9 NASB

It is your destruction, O Israel,
That *you are* against Me, against your <u>help</u>.

This is God's indictment through the prophet Hosea of any Israelite resisting God's help.

God designed women to be helpers, but not the kind of help Robin gives to Batman or an associate gives to the boss. No. We were imaged after God himself and given the ability to help the way he does, by fighting and winning battles.

The Need for Warrior-Helpers

Why did Adam need a warrior-helper? Apparently there was going to be a cosmic battle for good and evil, and Adam needed a co-warrior to fight with him. That's why Paul said:

Fight the good fight for the faith;
take hold of eternal life
that you were called to
and have made a good confession about
in the presence of many witnesses. (1 Tim. 6:12 HCSB)

Put on the full armor of God so that you can stand against the tactics of the Devil. For our battle is not against flesh and blood, but against the rulers, against the authorities, against the world powers of this darkness, against the spiritual forces of evil in the heavens. This is why you must take up the full armor of God, so that you may be able to resist in the evil day, and having prepared everything, to take your stand. (Eph. 6:11–13 HCSB)

Get your kilt on, sister, and paint half your face blue, as William Wallace did in the movie *Braveheart*, because we are going to be the generation our brothers look to when they need help in battle. Don't rein yourself in; reign the way Jesus would, as allies to our brothers and sisters.

Per the usual, the Bible has persuaded me and changed me in the process. Originally designed to guard the Garden, I have found a new purpose in life: to rule and multiply with my brothers in Christ as a warrior-helper. That much makes sense to me. But how? What is the best way to help? In part it will mean embracing the fact that, yes, of course, leading ladies can fit in supporting roles—Jesus's disciples know no other way.

Baffling his disciples, Jesus used a teachable moment to contrast the helper roles in God's kingdom against the leadership roles of the world that require a pecking order:

But Jesus called them together and said, "You know that the rulers in this world lord it over their people, and officials flaunt their authority over those under them. But among you it will be different. Whoever wants to be a leader among you must be your servant, and whoever wants to be first among you must become your slave. For even the Son of Man came not to be served but to serve others and to give his life as a ransom for many." (Matt. 20:25–28 NLT)

Dominant, charismatic leaders naturally draw followers looking for direction. There is something to be said for the ones at the top helping us find our way. But once we learn the ways of Jesus and the rhythms of his kingdom, we will follow his lead—bowing low, with our knees on the earth, to wash people's feet. Maybe we've made too much of certain personality types or leadership skills. It's time to welcome every human into a posture of humility.

John C. Maxwell knows a thing or two about leadership and is famous for saying, "Leadership isn't about titles, positions, or flowcharts. It is about one life influencing another."[6] Christ takes it one step further, encouraging his followers not only to throw out secular views of hierarchy but also to embrace self-sacrifice as the key to faith.

Living Proof

More specifically, being a good helper will mean emulating God himself, since he is the supreme Helper. Scripture describes how:

> Blessed are those whose help is the God of Jacob,
> whose hope is in the LORD their God. . . .
> He upholds the cause of the oppressed
> and gives food to the hungry.
> The LORD sets prisoners free,
> the LORD gives sight to the blind,
> the LORD lifts up those who are bowed down,
> the LORD loves the righteous.
> The LORD watches over the foreigner
> and sustains the fatherless and the widow,
> but he frustrates the ways of the wicked.
> The LORD reigns forever. (Ps. 146:5, 7–10 NIV)

The passage above is clear: Helpers uphold the cause of the oppressed and give food to the hungry. Helpers set prisoners free, give sight to the blind, lift up those who are bowed down, and love the righteous. Helpers watch over the foreigner, sustain the fatherless and the widow, and frustrate the ways of the wicked. Helpers reign.

The women around me provide countless examples of being good helpers. Ellie Langston noticed the children in her neighborhood needed after-school activities and access to the gospel, so she started Circle One ministry, a weekly service opportunity at her church. Kaitlyn Mullens started giving rides to refugees, which led to needing a van donated, which led to a full-fledged 501(c)(3) nonprofit called For the Nations reaching thousands of refugees. Becky Kiser goes into prisons with Bible studies she's written herself. Stephanie Giddens is teaching Muslim women how to sew and offering them self-sustaining jobs. Cessilye Smith started Abide Women's Health Services to improve birth outcomes in communities with the lowest quality care. Helping takes many forms based on everyone's unique personalities, circumstances, and availability. What if we started asking ourselves, Who is within my reach and needs my help?

This Is Us

Let's be the kind of women known for our character. When people talk about us, may they say that we protect people who need an advocate, that we are a stronghold and a shield to those who need a buffer from pain and suffering. When people talk about us, may they say we are always sticking up for people, speaking up for the voiceless, staying strong for the powerless. In the marketplace we champion our coworkers; at home we uphold the people we love; in society we build up . . . everyone.

As far as it's up to us, let's be women who fearlessly welcome refugees, generously meet the needs of the vulnerable, and confuse our enemies with kindness. When our names pop into someone's head, let's be known as the ones you can always count on for a helping hand. Helpers: This. Is. Us.

The outcast and the outsiders are *our* people. If you mess with the marginalized, you mess with us, the warrior-women fashioned to reign. The Enemy will have to go through us before hijacking the next generation. Forces of darkness will face us on the battlefield when the gospel work gets dangerous. And we are up for the challenge because we are the daughters of the church.

My client's hurtful words—"You can't help your husband the way God designed if you keep at it this way"—were not only untrue; they revealed that our understanding of a good helper determines the way we view and treat women.

If that client had pure motives, the better advice would have been to keep it up, not rein it in. He should have told me to "fan into flame" the gift of God inside me (2 Tim. 1:6 NIV), or to love God with my all (Mark 12:30), or to not grow weary of doing good (Gal. 6:9), or to "press on to take hold of that for which Christ Jesus took hold of me" (Phil. 3:12 NIV). He could have told me to check my motives, to make sure I wasn't trying to win the approval of the people around me instead of focusing on God's approval of my choices (Gal. 1:10). He could have cautioned me to be on the same page with my spouse while at the same time encouraging me to stay the course, if that is where God's called me.

His scribbly one-sentence Post-it Note said to "start in Genesis," and I'm glad it did. But I wish he had also told me to keep reading on to the end in Revelation, the last book of the Bible. Along the way I would have found countless examples of women in the Bible defying traditional roles to help the people around them in God's mission. I would have found the Great Commission in Matthew 28 that encourages all Christ-followers to go and make disciples of all nations, baptizing in the name of the Father, Son, and Holy Spirit and teaching those we convert all that Jesus commanded. It would have been clear that some of the duties we've limited to male clergy (evangelism, baptism, teaching) are really the responsibility of everyone who calls Jesus Lord. And I would have found that God's redemptive work would culminate in the end times, as described in Revelation, when he will re-create a new heaven and a new earth, the place where we will reign with Christ, a place where there are no stratified gender roles.

At the end of the day, I think the client preferred everyone to live in light of the Fall. I'm choosing to live knowing the Fall messed everything up, but that before the Fall, God designed women to be warriors, and in the end, the effects of the Fall will be no more. I don't want my life to reflect the way things usually are; I want my life to reflect the way things were supposed to be, and the way God says they are going to be.

Discussion Questions

- How would you define the role of women in our world?
- What about the word *ezer* impacted you most?
- Who are the people in your life you most need to help?
- What is the best way you can help them?
- How do you handle supporting roles?
- What would it look like to live in such a way that acknowledges the Fall but fights for the coming kingdom?

PART TWO

THE CALL TO

LOVE GOD

SIX

ALL YOUR HEART: DEVELOPING A HEART FOR GOD

> Blessed are the pure in heart,
> for they will see God.
>
> —MATTHEW 5:8 NIV

My grandmother knew the meaning of hard work in a way I never will; she knew survival. Often wondering how she would put food on the table, she fought the cycle of poverty and conquered it because she was tough as nails. Abuela passed away at the age of ninety-four, having lived independently in the same tiny house for fifty-three years in Harlingen, Texas. That house was the backdrop for long, hot, joy-filled summers eating homemade tortillas. No wonder I love carbs so much.

As a struggling single mother of two kids, she worked several jobs to make ends meet, including housekeeping and working at a cannery. One single light bulb illuminated their house until my mom was in high school, and they had to share a bathroom with other families in a little building separate from the rented houses where they stayed. Through the course of her life, two different men abandoned her, one while she was pregnant.

We demanded she stop mowing her own lawn when she reached her mid-eighties. Her insistence bordered on ridiculous. But we could never get her to quit gardening. I often wondered how a ninety-year-old would be able to get herself off the ground after hunching over to tend to her plants. When I asked her about it, she said, "*Mija*, I've been lifting myself up my whole life."

I'd like to believe her fierce independence and strength have passed down to me, but it's clear the green thumb skipped a couple of generations. I killed a basil plant last week, and it has joined an ever-growing graveyard of dead plants left in my wake.

Elvira Lopez knew the secrets to having good soil; she knew how to make things grow. Her legacy reminds me of our Cosmic Gardener, God Almighty, and how much of history, his story, unfolds before a garden backdrop. In chapter 1 we talked about Creation and the Fall that took place in the Garden of Eden, and the redemption of mankind at the garden tomb. But there will also be a re-creation when God makes the new heaven and new garden on earth. Clearly, we see a biblical theme meant to catch our attention. He, too, knows rich-soil secrets; his expertise is pruning and helping us bear fruit. It brings new significance to the phrase "tend your garden." And that's just what we have been doing together.

In the first section of this book, we cleared our theological gardens of weeds. Now we can plant the truth. Uprooting a gendered Great Commandment leaves us ready to absorb God's words as he always intended them. The mental energy we used to spend on worry is now freed up to embrace the reason we exist: to love God and love others. It's time to till the ground by digging deep into the Scriptures.

Breaking Down for a Breakthrough

I'm a newly converted Barre3 member, which means I'm working out at a Barre3 *studio* using the Barre3 *method*. I'm in shape, but I can barely walk. And though I can now sit and eat comfortably in my jeans without unzipping them, I have trouble getting into a seated position.

If you look up *Barre3*, the website will tell you it's a "full-body workout" that includes "sustained holds, micro-movements, and cardio bursts" that leave your body feeling balanced.[1] I agree. It might be the hardest type of exercise I've ever done, but it's also my favorite so far. Passionate as I am about sharing my newfound love with the women around me, Caleb, my five-year-old, has heard all about it maybe one too many times.

Our typical Saturday mornings include a trip to the studio for my Barre3 class with my little dude. One Saturday morning before my workout, I overheard Caleb telling his imaginary friend, "My mommy loves going to the bar." This is not the kind of thing you want the pastor's kid saying. Calling him into my room and getting on eye level, I asked, "Buddy, what did you just say?" With great confidence, Caleb said, "You love going to the bar and taking me with you." Seeing the horror on my face, he started to doubt himself. "You do love going to the bar, right, Mommy?" Wincing in emotional pain, I hesitantly asked, "Love, have you said that to anyone? Anyone at the church?" Next, I tried to explain some things that would ensure Daddy, the pastor at our church, still had a job the next Sunday.

"Buddy, buddy, pay attention. Mommy loves going to the barre *studio* for Barre3 classes. Going to a bar is different. Totally different thing. Please make sure, and this is really important, focus . . . focus, love. When you talk about Mommy going to the Barre, let's just call it the gym, okay?" Unfazed, he returned to his Legos. Meanwhile, I was reaching into the air and whispering to myself, "Literalism is dangerous."

You better believe I made sure to retell this story in several strategic ways in every potential place on the church campus. Laughing off the confusion, I attempted to get in front of the message: the pastor's wife frequents the bar with her kid. To anyone who has left our church due to this startling admission from my son, I'd like the record to show if you find me in a bar, it's usually because it's got the best burgers in the city. Just sayin'.

Approximately twenty minutes into a Barre3 workout, the instructors ask you to go one inch deeper into a hold. As your body starts to shake, they reassure you that this is normal. Coaching us to recognize the chaos entering our muscles, causing us to quiver, or in my case quake, they say to breathe through the hold. We all look like fools for thirty seconds, which feels like an hour, while our muscles break down for a breakthrough.

Now I am accustomed to pushing through and even enjoying the challenges in that sixty-minute workout. While sweat flies, my muscles are changing for the better. Even though I can anticipate the part of class that is going to hurt, I know building endurance is for my good. And I really appreciate the fact that all of the instructors in class make a point to remind us of what we are accomplishing physically by staying in a hold longer than we want. We can get through this, and we will be stronger for it.

Building Heart Strength

Paul spoke to this strength when he wrote to the Romans:

> Therefore, since we have been declared righteous by faith, we have peace with God through our Lord Jesus Christ. We have also obtained access through Him by faith into this grace in which we stand, and we rejoice in the hope of the glory of God. And not only that, but we also rejoice in our afflictions, because we know that affliction produces endurance, endurance produces proven character, and proven character produces hope. This hope will not disappoint us, because God's love has been poured out in our hearts through the Holy Spirit who was given to us. (Rom. 5:1–5 HCSB)

According to the Scriptures, we can come to a place in our faith when we rejoice in our pain. And that revelation happens when we remind ourselves that hardship produces endurance, endurance produces proven character, and proven character produces hope.

Building heart strength is a physical discipline for our bodies, but it can also teach us a sacred spiritual lesson about our heart for God. Facing the chaos of life, pushing through it, and enjoying the breakthrough that naturally follows is the kind of exercise our hearts need in order to thrive. And what I know for sure is that when we love God with our whole hearts, he will breathe into us the grit we need to cross the finish line even when we grow weary.

As I considered how we could live up to Jesus's call in Mark 12:30 to love God with all our hearts, I went to the Word of God for direction. Before looking up how often and in what setting the word *heart* was used in the Bible, I was expecting confirmation that ladies need to control their feelings, because I've grown up hearing how much more emotional women are than men and how much more relational we are than our brothers in Christ. While keeping my feelings in check and directing my affection toward Christ is a worthy goal, it's not the extent of loving God with all my heart. What I thought would be a lesson on tempering our feelings turned into a lesson on integrity. It's a lot more *Braveheart* than *Bridget Jones's Diary.*

I was surprised that even though the word *heart* appears more than a thousand times in the Bible, it rarely describes just our feelings or one of our internal organs. Instead, many of the authors of Scripture use the term more broadly to mean "our truest inner selves." Think about that. Our truest inner selves can sometimes be buried beneath our insecurities, our talents, or the opinions of others, or they may even contrast what we say we believe. When authors of Scripture used the word *heart*, they intended for us to envision the raw, plain truth about our whole lives.

What's Driving Your Heart?

I sifted through commentaries and lexicons to find that the meaning of *heart* in the Bible includes our whole personality and disposition, with an emphasis on reason and will. The best way

I could summarize my findings on the word is that our heart is the driving force behind our actions.[2] Loving God with all our hearts is not just feeling love toward God or redirecting misguided feelings back to God. It's about letting our love for him determine how we live.

When Jesus asked the scribes, "Why are you thinking these things in your hearts?" (Mark 2:8 HCSB), isn't it interesting that he asked about *thinking* rather than *feeling*? I usually separate those two into different categories, because lots of personality tests make thinking and feeling a binary choice. The truth is, thinking and feeling are deeply intertwined. Jesus's point is that our thought life and emotional well-being are interconnected.

Later, Jesus explained that out of people's hearts come evil actions: "For from within, out of people's hearts, come evil thoughts, sexual immoralities, thefts, murders, adulteries, greed, evil actions, deceit, promiscuity, stinginess, blasphemy, pride, and foolishness. All these evil things come from within and defile a person" (Mark 7:21–23 HCSB).

What a list! Jesus is saying our behavior reveals the contents of our hearts.

In Luke, Jesus said, "Good people bring good things out of the good they stored in their hearts. But evil people bring evil things out of the evil they stored in their hearts. People speak the things that are in their hearts" (Luke 6:45 NCV).

Verse after verse points to the fact that our behavior reveals our authentic selves, which is the meaning of *heart* in the Bible. Loving God with all our hearts is so much more than Jesus-focused mushy-gushy stuff. It's about loving God with our truest inner selves and letting that love shine through our lives and determine our actions. But to accomplish that, we have to persevere. That's why the word *heart* comes up several times when the authors of the Bible talk about how hard it is to keep going.

Paul and Timothy, two New Testament church planters, wrote a letter to the Christians in Corinth. It's a gut-wrenching message about faithfulness to God's priorities in the midst of harsh adversity. Coupling negative emotions about their difficult circumstances with profound, timeless, and uplifting truths about God, it almost feels as though Paul and Timothy can't decide whether they are depressed or joyful. Then you realize they are living in the inevitable tension where suffering and celebration coexist. Similar to my workouts, life is fun and hard and sometimes both at once.

Paul and Timothy described their suffering to the Corinthians this way: "For we don't want you to be unaware, brothers, of our affliction that took place in Asia: we were completely overwhelmed—beyond our strength—so that we even despaired of life" (2 Cor. 1:8 HCSB).

They felt completely overwhelmed, beyond their strength, and at times despairing of life. I can certainly relate. But they also spoke about the "God of all comfort, who comforts us in all our troubles so that we may be able to comfort those experiencing any trouble with the comfort with which we ourselves are comforted by God" (2 Cor. 1:3–4 NET).

While Paul and Timothy first described themselves and others as extremely troubled and overwhelmed by grief, they then transitioned into the happy topic of the Holy Spirit's work in Christians:

> But we have this treasure in earthen vessels, so that the surpassing greatness of the power will be of God and not from

ourselves; *we are* afflicted in every way, but not crushed; perplexed, but not despairing; persecuted, but not forsaken; struck down, but not destroyed; always carrying about in the body the dying of Jesus, so that the life of Jesus also may be manifested in our body. For we who live are constantly being delivered over to death for Jesus' sake, so that the life of Jesus also may be manifested in our mortal flesh. So death works in us, but life in you. (2 Cor. 4:7–12 NASB)

Paul said we are pressured but not crushed, perplexed but not despairing, persecuted but not in despair, struck down but not destroyed. And I call that life. Real life. Paul and Timothy's letter to the Corinthians encourages principled living to those running out of steam. Exactly what will be required of us if we take Jesus up on his command to love him with all our hearts.

Don't Lose Heart

Paul and Timothy knew that even in light of the remarkable things God does on our behalf, it's easy to lose our motivation to keep on keeping on. To those living in that tough, real-life place, Paul encouraged, "Do not lose heart":

Therefore we do not lose heart. Though outwardly we are wasting away, yet inwardly we are being renewed day by day. For our light and momentary troubles are achieving for us an eternal glory that far outweighs them all. So we fix our eyes not on what is seen, but on what is unseen, since what is seen is temporary, but what is unseen is eternal. (2 Cor. 4:16–18 NIV)

Some Bible versions translate the phrase "don't lose heart" as "do not give up" or "don't grow weary"—don't become discouraged or be spiritless, despairing, exhausted, or faint. I wonder if you feel weary today. I wonder if you know all too well the bone-tired exhaustion that comes right before we throw in the towel. God knew we would face the kind of discouragement that makes us consider quitting. That's why he made sure in his Word to include several reminders not to lose heart. He knew we would be tempted to.

Get Moving

Are you starting to lose heart? I wonder if God is stirring something in you right now. Maybe it's clear that your inner truest self needs to focus on God. Maybe up until now your relationship with God has been surface level, or maybe you're trying to hide something from him or from your loved ones or even from yourself. That's the place where it's easiest to give up on God and the people of God. Because there is nothing more tiring than knowing you need to get your life right and all the hard work it will take to get there. But how do you get the strength you need to keep going?

Pray

It's so important to keep a conversation going with God. Always "pray that the eyes of your heart may be enlightened in order that you may know the hope to which he has called you" (Eph. 1:18 NIV). When we talk to God, our prayers do not fall on deaf ears. He is not taking a nap or more concerned about someone else. He is listening to us. Jesus wants us to take heart, not lose it. This endurance we need to love God with our truest inner selves is only possible when we persist in prayer, because when we pray, his peace "which transcends all understanding, will guard your hearts and your minds in Christ Jesus" (Phil. 4:7 NIV).

Get into the Word

Another important exercise for our spiritual hearts is immersing ourselves in God's living Word. It offers instruction and encouragement, and it builds endurance that we need to keep going. The apostle Peter said, "'The word of the Lord endures forever.' And this is the word that was preached to you" (1 Peter 1:25 NIV).

Join a Team

Part of the reason I joined Barre3 in the first place was to appease my licensed professional counselor. After my father passed away, my heart felt as if it had been ripped out of my chest. There were so many things about my dad, myself, and God that I knew to be true, but my actions were not reflecting those truths. On a surface level I was managing my grief well, but underneath was inexpressible hurt that I didn't want to deal with because I knew it would be a lot of work. It was hard to apply the Great Commandment in that season.

My counselor suggested that, in addition to all sorts of other ways to work through my grief, I needed to be doing physical exercise. I never imagined the spiritual lessons I would learn about loving God with all my heart through cardio strength training and the help of the right instructors in my workout classes.

You see, the best part of Barre3 workouts is the instructors. I went to social media to describe the stages of appreciation for our instructors, and here's how I summarized the emotional roller-coaster workouts: "First, you see the instructor and you think, *Oh, she's smiley; she's here to help me.* And then you get done with warm-up and you think, *This lady is taking it out on us, whatever it may be.* And then by the time she puts us in those micro-movements, you think, *Get away from me, lady; why do you torture us?* But by the end of class, as we rebalance ourselves and lie still to relax, I remind myself, *She's so great; she really cares about my well-being; she's here to help me.*"

In addition to doing the hard work alongside us, they know just when to tell us to keep going. My instructors are well practiced at seeing when I am really feeling the burn, and that's when they tell me to breathe. And many times they ask me to consider going one inch deeper, move a little faster, or sit tight for a few more seconds. In fact, they usually make a point in their coaching to talk about the fact that relief is coming, so give it all you've got in the moment. In essence, they've been telling me not to hold back when things get hard. It's because that is how we develop physical and mental toughness. They remind us that we can carry these lessons into our everyday lives. Because in real life we face challenges and we can get through those too. While all I want to do is find a way out of the discomfort, my workouts have taught me that additional reps are going to make me stronger.

The same is true for our spiritual cardio. As we seek to strengthen our hearts for God, we should build a team of trusted godly Bible teachers, mentors, or friends to walk alongside us to speak into our ears, to keep us moving, to help us hold on when our poses get shaky. In the stressful and downright defeating circumstances in my life, when I can feel the burn, metaphorically speaking, I first turn to Jesus. He is our most reliable, trusted chief Instructor when it comes to the matters of the heart. His Holy Spirit is coaching us through the hardest parts of life, reminding us not to give up. He will supply all the encouragement we need.

Developing a heart for God will require some hard work, but it's how we build strength and add depth to our spiritual lives. So don't lose heart. That muscle-shaking, strengthening pose will serve to strengthen your character and deepen your faith further than you imagined you could go.

Discussion Questions

- How have you experienced the messages from society or church culture that women are the heart and soul of our communities?
- Before reading the chapter, what was your view on loving God with all your heart?
- Spiritually speaking, how would you diagnose your heart health?
- Describe your plan for strengthening your spiritual heart for God.
- What part of your life tempts you to lose heart?

SEVEN

ALL YOUR SOUL: PRAISING GOD WHEN LIFE GETS REAL

And Mary said,

"My soul exalts the Lord,
and my spirit has begun to
rejoice in God my Savior."

—LUKE 1:46–47 NET

My husband is indifferent to music, which kills me. I saw this in action for the first time on our second first date. Yes, we had two. The first was incredible, but then he left for summer camp and, yada yada yada, we had to start over again with a second "first date" months later. That time the stakes were higher. I *really* wanted to date Aaron Armstrong on our first date, but on the second, I knew I wanted to marry him.

We were on our way to a baseball game, jamming to a U2 song in the car, when both of our bodies started swaying.

Shouting over Bono's unrivaled voice, I said, "I love this song!" Aaron responded, "Yeah, it's good! Who sings it?" We both started laughing, but mine was nervous laughter. Did he not *recognize* Bono's voice? Was that possible?

While giving him a side-eye I asked, "I'm sorry, what?" I started pointing to the radio, explaining, "This is U2, man." He gave me a shoulder shrug and a playful smile, so I asked, "Are you messing with me?" Next, I tried jogging his memory with facts. U2 is the greatest rock band of all time. B-O-N-O, the lead singer, pastors me with his song sermons, and he's the guy that wears the glasses . . . onstage. He's basically alleviating poverty by himself. Facts. But Aaron didn't care. And maybe *care* is too lenient. Perhaps it's just flat disobedience to the Lord to not recognize and celebrate the U2 catalog of musical greatness.

Remember, at this point I thought he was going to be my husband. I mean, *he* didn't know that yet, but in my mind it was a done deal. We would forever be Team Armstrong. But now, after months of pining and finally getting to the second first date that was always meant to be, I started to ask, "Lord, is this U2 situation a deal breaker?" Ultimately, I decided—in all of my twenty-year-old wisdom—that I could fix this. I could change him, and the truth would set him free.

In the seventeen years since that moment, as you could have accurately predicted, Aaron still doesn't recognize U2 songs or Bono's voice, because he doesn't care much about either. If you ask him, he'll tell you he's improving. But we just saw U2 live again last year, and while Bono was belting out "In the Name of Love," the song that never fails to make me cry, Aaron leaned over to jokingly tell me he didn't know they sang *that* song. I just rolled my eyes and said, "Aaron, are you dead inside? Don't you have a soul?"

Joking aside, my sarcasm reveals something intuitive about the concept of soul. We know it's connected to life. We know that all living human beings have a soul, and some Bible experts would say we don't just *have* a soul; we *are* a living soul.[1] They are one and the same. Many times in the Old Testament, scholars actually translate the word *soul* as "life" because the two are inseparable.

The Holman Treasury of Key Bible Words says, "If we properly understand the profound meaning encapsulated in the word 'soul,' then the greatest of all commandments carries a far deeper significance than a surface reading would allow. . . . We should love the Lord with the very fiber of our being, with everything that makes us human!"[2] If Jesus guides us to love him with all our souls, then he's looking for women to love him through all aspects of our lives—the good, the bad, and the ugly.

A Model of Faith

If any lady in the Scriptures exemplifies what it means to love God with all her soul, it's Mary, Jesus's mother. According to professor Timothy Ralston, she ranks as the fourth-most-described person in the New Testament behind Jesus, Paul, and Peter.[3] All four gospel writers give us part of Mary's story to show us she's a model disciple of Jesus, a humble servant of God, and fully committed to her faith.

One of the gospel writers, Luke, does something unique with the birth announcement of Jesus. He brings us into the narrative in such a way that we can experience it from a woman's perspective, and he allows the story to be a woman-only scene. Both are rare in the Bible. The only other recorded times the people of God have heard a woman singing praises for salvation are through Miriam, Moses's sister, who led the people of God in worship after crossing the Red Sea and receiving deliverance from the Egyptians (Ex. 15:21); Deborah, God's appointed judge and prophet, who helped Barak defeat the enemy (Judg. 5); and Hannah, mother of the prophet Samuel, the last judge to rule Israel (1 Sam. 2:1–10). Luke's gospel should be a mile marker for those of us pursuing God. It should remind us that God gives voice to women, and Mary is joining an exclusive group of women of the Old Testament used by God as his agents of salvation.

The book of Luke tells the story of a young Jewish girl named Mary who was engaged to marry a man named Joseph (Luke 1). The angel Gabriel was sent by God to Nazareth, where Mary was living at the time, to announce to Mary that, although she was a virgin, the Holy Spirit would come upon her and she would conceive and give birth to the Messiah. He went on to explain that, although she was deeply troubled by his statement, she should not be afraid. Okay, angel. He explained this turn of events was a blessing from God. Mary's son was going to be the Son of God, and his name would be Jesus.

Imagine with me that you are a young teenage girl confronted by an angel who explains that you will give birth to the Messiah. I wonder what it's like to realize you'll be the conduit, the physical means, for God to accomplish deliverance for all people. What a revelation! What a heavy responsibility!

Richard Bauckham's book *Gospel Women: Studies of the Named Women in the Gospels* explains:

> The events that transpire in Luke 1 are not matters of purely personal and private significance . . . rather they constitute

a turning point in the story of God's people Israel and the fulfillment of his purposes for them. They are laden with the promises and hopes of the past and pregnant with the future in which these promises and hopes will at last be fulfilled.[4]

Let Mary's situation settle a minute. She literally delivered the gospel. And that is what all Christians are supposed to be doing—delivering the good news.

After Mary processed her fear in the presence of the angel, and after she thought through the miracle, she began praising God:

> My soul proclaims the greatness of the Lord,
> and my spirit has rejoiced in God my Savior,
> because He has looked with favor
> on the humble condition of His slave.
> Surely, from now on all generations
> will call me blessed,
> because the Mighty One
> has done great things for me,
> and His name is holy.
> His mercy is from generation to generation
> on those who fear Him.
> He has done a mighty deed with His arm;
> He has scattered the proud
> because of the thoughts of their hearts;
> He has toppled the mighty from their thrones
> and exalted the lowly.
> He has satisfied the hungry with good things
> and sent the rich away empty.
> He has helped His servant Israel,

mindful of His mercy,

just as He spoke to our ancestors,

to Abraham and his descendants forever. (Luke 1:46–55 HCSB)

Much of what Mary sang about in her famous anthem, known as the Magnificat, comes from an Old Testament prophecy in Isaiah 61, then later in the New Testament when Jesus quoted the same verses in Luke 4. Speaking of the future Messiah, Isaiah prophesied:

The Spirit of the Lord GOD is on Me,

because the LORD has anointed Me

to bring good news to the poor.

He has sent Me to heal the brokenhearted,

to proclaim liberty to the captives

and freedom to the prisoners;

to proclaim the year of the LORD's favor

and the day of our God's vengeance;

to comfort all who mourn,

to provide for those who mourn in Zion;

to give them a crown of beauty instead of ashes,

festive oil instead of mourning,

and splendid clothes instead of despair. (Isa. 61:1–3 HCSB)

In the New Testament, Luke wrote of Jesus:

He came to Nazareth, where He had been brought up. As usual, He entered the synagogue on the Sabbath day and stood up to read. The scroll of the prophet Isaiah was given to Him, and unrolling the scroll, He found the place where it was written:

> The Spirit of the Lord is on Me,
> because He has anointed Me
> to preach good news to the poor.
> He has sent Me
> to proclaim freedom to the captives
> and recovery of sight to the blind,
> to set free the oppressed,
> to proclaim the year of the Lord's favor.

He then rolled up the scroll, gave it back to the attendant, and sat down. And the eyes of everyone in the synagogue were fixed on Him. He began by saying to them, "Today as you listen, this Scripture has been fulfilled." (Luke 4:16–21 HCSB)

(Drops microphone to stage.)

My brain can barely compute the significance of this moment, and I wish I had been present to see the faces of those within earshot. A Jewish reader would have had their hair blown back to hear that Isaiah's message of freedom for the poor, oppressed, enslaved, brokenhearted, despairing, and mourning could come to fruition through a person, Jesus, rather than a season of time in the Jewish agricultural calendar called Jubilee. And it would have been all the more shocking that a young virgin named Mary would fulfill the prophecies.

Mary's reaction and song astound me. The birth announcement would have brought, at best, an unplanned disruption to her life. At worst, a future filled with shame, rejection, and poverty, especially if Joseph could not understand. Even so, Mary chose to lift up her voice to worship in spite of her uncertain future and very scary present. Mary knew how to celebrate God's faithfulness even when her life got real, real complicated. And her example can teach us about loving God with all our souls.

What I want to know is, where did Mary find this kind of faith in the moment? And why did she respond the way she did?

Our Source of Solid Faith

I think Mary was immediately able to obey and begin praising God because her faith was solid. She was ready to believe God in season and out. Her circumstances didn't dictate her level of faith. She believed the slaves would be set free, even if at the moment she was still a lowly servant herself. She had faith that the hungry were going to be fed, even though she saw poverty all around her. She trusted that the brokenhearted would find joy again, even though her own life plan was going to be redirected. Mary knew the God who could accomplish all of this. When he showed up and revealed the next steps in his plan, she was filled with faith, even though her soul must have been troubled.

Mary's story may be very different from your own, but I bet you know what it's like to have an uncertain future or a scary present. And I want to remind you that now's the time to stay connected to God. If your life is hard, in a way you can't describe to even your closest friends or family, guess what? Jesus will understand.

He wants us to trust him when we get a promotion at work, when we fail miserably on a project, and when we slog through an ordinary nine-to-five job. He calls us to enjoy him on an emotional mountaintop and in the pit of despair, and even when we feel blah. He wants stay-at-home moms to praise him when the baby takes his first steps and when the child comes home from school with a failing grade, and during the long trudge of sleepless nights and early-morning wake-up calls.

God desires our companionship when we are easy to talk to, when we feel like giving him the silent treatment, or when we repeat the same old conversation we had with him yesterday. In fact, God longs for us to bring him all our highs, lows, and everything in between. To rejoice in God through it all is the kind of commitment God seeks. Loving God with all our souls is praising him through every season of life.

Praising with Broken Hallelujahs

And spoiler alert: that doesn't mean our praise will always feel glad. Sometimes we will lament. The book of Lamentations is devoted to hopeful sorrow, bursting with pain—rip-your-heart-out, tear-your-clothes, lift-your-fist-to-God pain. Squirming through depressing prayers, I found myself shocked and encouraged by the author's authenticity.

Listen to how serious inner turmoil sounds in the Bible:

> My soul has been deprived of peace;
> I have forgotten what happiness is.
> Then I thought: My future is lost,
> as well as my hope from the LORD.
> Remember my affliction and my homelessness,
> the wormwood and the poison.
> I continually remember them
> and have become depressed. (Lam. 3:17–20 HCSB)

Crying out to our Savior with hurt and anger is not only permissible; it's an act of worship. As our tears fall and our heads hang low, our cries directed to the living God prove our faith; we believe he exists and that reaching out to him will ease our suffering. Faith *is* for the faint of heart. Hope *is* for the souls deprived of peace.

My friend Tanisha spent thirteen years in an emotionally abusive and adulterous marriage. Despite her best efforts for reconciliation, she's out of that harmful situation now. I watched and marveled at Tanisha's strength through it all. Although she felt stuck for a long time in a seemingly hopeless situation, time and time again she'd tell me she had found new ways to praise God in her trials, and she had no problem telling him how hard this had been for her.

Listening to her pray was life changing for me because I knew all that was going on behind closed doors. She would confess her deep pain to God, venting her anger, yet circle back around into praise, all within a few minutes' prayer time. I watched her celebrate her friends' anniversaries and healthy marriages with genuine appreciation for their joy, and I watched tears roll down her face as she explained her own marriage was coming to an end.

Over the course of our friendship, I've witnessed her embrace life-altering change with dignity and courage in her role as a single mom, facing hardships with lament while maintaining her conviction that the best is yet to come. She shows me what it looks like to trust God completely. She would be the first to tell you she doesn't know what the future holds, but she knows who holds her future. Tanisha loves God with all her soul because she anchors her life in the promise that one day God will make all things new and, in the meantime, he's here now.

Soulful living doesn't mean we spend our days humming happy tunes about the good in our lives, acting continuously downcast about the bad, or mourning the ugly. Soulful living encompasses all of that and everything in between. Aspiring to fulfill the greatest commandment means honoring God when life gets real, through thick and thin.

My father struggled with a lifetime of substance abuse, depression, and chronic pain. He passed in 2017 as a result of a suicide attempt, and his death inaugurated the hardest and darkest season of my life so far. Watching him wither away and lose hope devastated me. Even now as I try to write about his story, words fail me. My dad took his life, and I'm still reeling. My family is still grieving because grief will be an unwanted part of our lives until Jesus returns and restores to us what has been lost. For this season in life, I needed examples of stories like Mary's and Tanisha's more than ever before. I needed to be reminded we can keep our faith and step into God's plan even though our souls are troubled.

Father's Day rolled around just weeks after he died. I could barely make it into the sanctuary for church before the tears started flowing. You'd think lifting up my hands during worship that day would have been impossible. It was terribly hard; I'll give you that. All I had was broken hallelujahs and prayers of lament, but I sent them up anyway. Because here's what I know for sure. Things are not as they should be right now, and I'm not happy about the way they turned out. To clarify, death is our enemy, and no one should experience what my father went through. But I get to see him again, and I'm holding on to that. Until then, in this in-between time, I know Jesus helps me keep the faith, although it's harder than I could have ever imagined.

When we got the call to go say goodbye to my dad for the last time, Aaron and I rushed to the hospital. The two of us, both communicators by trade, rode together in silence, speechless. We focused all our energy on what we would say to my dad in these last few critical moments. I remember texting Glenn, one of my spiritual fathers, to let him know it was time for me to say goodbye, and he texted back, "If you can, forgive him." I lost it. I knew Glenn was right. And I knew what would help me prepare for this unspeakable moment—a song of lament.

I quickly pulled out my phone to play U2's song "Sometimes You Can't Make It on Your Own" as Aaron sped us to the hospital. It is said that Bono wrote that song for his own father, Bob, and sang it for the first time at his funeral. I don't know if that is true, but I know that ever since I understood the words, more than ten years ago now, I knew it would be my song for my father. It seems to me the song expresses a child's wish for a parent to get help. Hopeful lament comes through the lyrics and voices my own wish for my dad. As the song played, Aaron reached over to hold my hand. He gave me a quick side glance stained with tears, because this time Aaron recognized Bono's voice—glory to God, he works miracles! That tiny moment broke the silence and reminded me that God is in the details.

By God's grace I got to tell my dad goodbye. I got to say my piece. No one prepares you for the agony that follows turning off the machines in a hospital room, and no one can explain the peace that follows after someone passes into the arms of Jesus. As I left his hospital room, I gave him one last hug and told him I'd see him on the other side.

I realize, on a very personal level, that loving God with all our souls at times seems impossible. At best it seems daunting.

But I have good news for you. Sometimes loving God with all your soul means rejoicing in faith, as Mary did, that God's promises are coming to pass. Sometimes loving God with all your soul means celebrating God's faithfulness, as Tanisha did, when life doesn't turn out the way we expected. And sometimes loving God with all our souls means crying out to him in lament, as the author of Lamentations did.

Whether you are in a high or low season, now is always the time to praise God with all your soul.

Discussion Questions

- Describe a time when you experienced an uncertain future or a scary present. How did God help you through it?
- Knowing that many Bible translators use the words "life" and "soul" interchangeably, how does that influence how you think about God's Great Commandment to love him with all your soul?
- How could the church cultivate compassion for people who have troubled souls?
- Why do you think Mary's soul was able to proclaim the greatness of the Lord just moments after receiving frightening and life-altering news?
- What are some of God's promises to us that should comfort our souls?
- How can you celebrate God's faithfulness when life doesn't turn out the way you expected?
- What does it look like when you lament?

EIGHT

ALL YOUR MIND: STAYING OPEN TO NEW IDEAS

> He began to speak boldly in the synagogue. After Priscilla and Aquila heard him, they took him home and explained the way of God to him more accurately.
>
> —ACTS 18:26 HCSB

In May 2003, Aaron and I packed up our one-bedroom efficiency apartment in College Station, Texas. With room to spare, we fit all of our belongings into a tiny U-Haul truck and moved to Dallas for grad school. With the windows up and the AC blasting, we prioritized our punch list: find jobs, live as frugally as possible, and save, save, save.

Lucky for us, the same year that Big D became home, we discovered Apartment Life, a ministry that offers discounted rent to teams of two people willing to serve as apartment chaplains. Their concept was genius. Reducing resident turnover makes more profit for a residential complex because keeping residents is much cheaper than finding new ones. Retention depends upon a sense of community. Caring for one's neighbors dramatically increases the likelihood that a resident will stay longer.

In exchange for budget-friendly rent prices, we planned community events and provided spiritual support. God placed us in an area brimming with young professionals. He knew ministry to our peers would be fruitful and that we needed to find friends. The work was rewarding, in every sense of the word.

One of the residents who enjoyed our socials was Dawn. She pitched in often, helping us set up and tear down, especially when Aaron got caught at work and I was left to manage the events by myself. She unknowingly became an invaluable part of our ministry. Now a dear friend, Dawn continues to show up to support me when I need her most.

Seeing the overwhelming crowd of hungry people at one of our resident dinners, she introduced herself to me and asked to help slice the bread. I gladly accepted and practically wanted to kiss this helpful stranger. Bonding over shared experiences, we got dinner ready for our guests and talked about attending the same university, sharing the same major, taking classes with several of the same professors, and how we'd both be ending up in sales. We could have talked for hours that night had it not been for refilling empty glasses and cooking second helpings of spaghetti noodles.

During that first conversation, Dawn asked me about our role in the community. In the middle of my explaining that Aaron and I served as event coordinators and were available for anyone who needed prayer or encouragement, she set down her plate to make what was obviously going to be an important point. She did not ever want to talk about God. Never. We could talk about anything else, and she wanted to be my friend, but Jesus was off-limits. As time passed, I continued to respect the boundary she had set up. The problem was, as our friendship grew, Dawn kept asking about God.

Several times a week she and I would walk laps around the block to process our work stress and relationships. More often than not, she had questions about my faith, and eventually she started asking for prayer. Watching the Holy Spirit soften her heart to the things of God ministered to me. Over time she not only felt comfortable with a whole conversation about spiritual stuff but also initiated those conversations. Opening her mind to receiving new ideas, God taught Dawn that he loved her. These days we get a real kick out of reminiscing about the first time we met because she's busy raising a godly young man, sharing her faith with her coworkers, and investing in her local church.

While God was inviting Dawn into his love, he was reminding me that he holds the power to change our minds. The apostle Paul talked about this when he wrote, "Now God has revealed these things to us by the Spirit, for the Spirit searches everything, even the depths of God" (1 Cor. 2:10 HCSB). Paul goes on to say that the Spirit explains spiritual things to spiritual people. Unbelievers do not get it until God replaces their minds with his own. Dawn has always been brilliant, a caring friend, and involved in her community. But she's a different person now because Jesus transformed her mind.

Redeemed: Heart, Soul, and Mind

On a weekend, as we were loitering around the front office to meet new residents, Irina was helping her boyfriend, Jeff, move into our apartment complex. A significant part of our ministry involved making newbies feel welcome and lightening their load, so we knocked on Jeff's door to offer help. I'll never forget Irina opening the door with a box in her arms and a smile that lit up her face. You know those delightful kinds of people? Well, that's her. Little did I know that encounter would lead us into a life-long friendship. After several flights up and down the stairs with furniture, we got Jeff moved into his new digs. When Irina tells the story, she emphasizes her concern about the two strangers likely planning to rob her unsuspecting boyfriend on move-in day. Apparently, she told Jeff to keep an eye on us.

The Lord orchestrated our proximity to them, placing them on the other side of the hall just one floor below us in a massive fifteen-building complex. Panting and high-fiving over the last truckload making its way upstairs, we asked if they would want to double date. The rest is history. Jeff knew the Lord, but Irina wasn't sure about Jesus. Spending weekends together trying out restaurants and taking in the latest festivals, we started sharing our lives and our faith with them.

As the last ones to leave the restaurant one night, I remember Irina pulling me aside and questioning the best time to come to faith in Christ. My answer was: right now! Encouraging her not to wait on such an important decision but sensing she was not looking to commit on the spot, I told her to consider making her decision that night. We waved goodbye and then Aaron and I prayed all the way home.

The next morning we had a red blinking light on our answering machine. Irina had left us a tearful voice mail. As her voice cracked, she did her best to explain that for the first time late the night before, she'd put her faith in Christ. Sniffling through her story, she kept repeating, "Everything makes sense now." Aaron and I were jumping up and down, probably waking up our downstairs neighbors.

Later in the week, Irina described in more detail the moments she surrendered her life to Jesus. She said it was the feeling of being washed clean, like a bucket of warm water from heaven pouring over her head, saturating her new life. It was the Holy Spirit doing the work of filling and sealing her life. Soon after making her decision for Christ, she left for work and came upon a one-way sign that was pointing in the wrong direction. She may have seen the sign several times before, but on that first day as a new Christian she said it symbolized her past.

Irina's conversion displays the radical shift we experience when God gives us the mind of Christ. Her transformation did not involve just comprehending the basics of Christianity. Everything in her life now made sense. In her own words, Irina described what the Bible promises Christians in 1 Corinthians 2:16: "We have the mind of Christ." In addition to giving us a new heart willing to do the right thing and a soul able to celebrate God when life gets real, God also redeems our minds.

Mindful Women of God

If being able to love God with all our hearts and all our souls feels like a challenging concept, fully understanding what it means to love God with all our minds might be even more convicting. Scripture says, "We demolish arguments and every high-minded thing that is raised up against the knowledge of God, taking every thought captive to obey Christ" (2 Cor. 10:4–5 HCSB). It sounds a bit like thought-life fight club.

In the Scriptures, *mind* means what you'd think it does— thoughts and perception. The struggle comes when it moves past those things and on into our opinions. And when those opinions are errant, it means we must accept that we have been thinking incorrectly. How else can I say this? Nobody likes being wrong.

The apostle Paul painted a stark contrast between the unregenerate mind and someone living with eternity on the brain. Writing to the church in Rome he said, "Those who live according to the flesh think about the things of the flesh, but those who live according to the Spirit, about the things of the Spirit" (Rom. 8:5 HCSB).

Then he explained the comparison:

> For the mind-set of the flesh is death, but the mind-set of the Spirit is life and peace. For the mind-set of the flesh is hostile to God because it does not submit itself to God's law, for it is unable to do so. Those who are in the flesh cannot please God. (vv. 6–8)

The passage describes people prior to conversion as being enemies of God in their minds, hostile toward God, and feeling as though God is against them. Sin's deceitfulness corrupts them.

But Jesus-followers enjoy a new-covenant mind where God's laws are put in their brains along with the power to obey them, conviction about right and wrong, a sense of belonging, openness to friendship with God, and renewal of their reasoning and perceptions.

Although Irina is one of the kindest, sincerest, and most intelligent people you will ever meet, she will admit to you that before coming to faith in Christ, her mind-set was not to obey God's instructions, and she felt powerless to do so when she had the inclination to listen to God's Word. Paul told us why. The mind-set of the flesh doesn't bring us life, and it keeps us from connecting with God. But Paul goes on to explain that Christians don't have that mind-set anymore. He says, "You, however, are not in the flesh, but in the Spirit, since the Spirit of God lives in you" (Rom. 8:9 HCSB).

Paul used another passage of Scripture to reemphasize the comparison between the mind of someone who doesn't know Christ as Savior and someone who does. He said it this way: "You took off your former way of life, the old self that is corrupted by deceitful desires; you are being renewed in the spirit of your minds; you put on the new self, the one created according to God's likeness in righteousness and purity of the truth" (Eph. 4:22–24 HCSB).

"A former way of life" is referring to living without a relationship with God through faith in Christ. Paul described this lifestyle as being corrupted by deceitful desires.

Irina could tell you that even with the best intentions, her old way of thinking undermined her faith in God and kept her from absorbing God's Word as true. But after she became a Christian, the Spirit of God renewed her mind, a concept we will come back to in a few minutes. Irina's conversion gave her access to righteousness and purity that wasn't possible before.

As we become more and more like Christ, as his mind replaces more of our own, we will find that our behavior will change too. Paul continued his letter by describing what that process would look like: "All bitterness, anger and wrath, shouting and slander must be removed from you, along with all malice. And be kind and compassionate to one another, forgiving one another, just as God also forgave you in Christ" (Eph. 4:31–32 HCSB).

Without the mind of Christ, forgiveness in the name of Jesus is not possible. If our job is to forgive, we will need Jesus's brainwaves to do it, since he is the one who offers true forgiveness.

Women with Their Heads on Straight

I have heard people criticize women in the Gospels for their overly emotional responses to situations with Jesus. A closer look proves in each case that women who have been assumed to be hysterical, impassioned, or sentimental actually thought correctly about spiritual matters. Women have no advantage over men when applying their minds to Christ, because both genders have access to the Holy Spirit, which enlightens us to understand truth. But I will say, it seems the Gospel writers, under the inspiration of the Spirit, made a concerted effort to highlight female disciples making accurate judgment calls based on logical thought processes and astute comprehension of events. I think the Bible levels the playing field for women seeking to love God with all their minds.

For instance, in John 11 we read of Mary and Martha's brother, Lazarus, who fell deathly ill. Knowing that Jesus could fix the situation, the sisters pursued Jesus with the news. Strangely, he did not respond the way Mary and Martha would have hoped, delaying his arrival so long that Lazarus died. Four days after Lazarus's burial, Jesus arrived in the town of Bethany to find Mary and Martha distraught with grief, and understandably so. Their brother was dead.

The Scriptures describe Martha catching wind of Jesus's arrival in town. Taking off to meet him, unable to wait one more minute to confront his indifference for their pain, she lamented, "Lord, if You had been here, my brother wouldn't have died" (John 11:21 HCSB). Martha spoke the truth. We can't know for sure how she said those words or what her tone communicated about her emotions, but we read John's quotes to find that Martha knew what she was talking about.

Most of the sermons I've heard on this moment in our faith history revolve around Martha's sensitive response in her sorrow. We might even replay the events in our head to assume Martha was accusing Jesus with anger when she said, "If You had been here, my brother wouldn't have died." But her comments are also another way of saying, "Your presence brings life," which is an admission of faith. If Jesus had been present when Lazarus fell ill, he could have healed him; that is true.

Jesus proclaimed to Martha the life-altering news: he is the resurrection and the life, and anyone who believes in him, even if they die, will live. And then he questioned Martha on this new information. "Do you believe this?" (v. 26 HCSB). Martha confessed, "I believe You are the Messiah, the Son of God, who comes into the world" (v. 27 HCSB). Our hearts should quicken as we read about the saving grace of Jesus making sense to someone. What a work of the Spirit.

Next, Jesus requested Mary's presence. Rushing to Jesus,

Mary fell at her Savior's feet and told him the same thing Martha had: "Lord, if You had been here, my brother would not have died!" (v. 32 HCSB). Comforting each other and hovering over their brother's dead body, the sisters had likely traded their sentiments during their lament.

The text points out Mary was crying (v. 33) while she threw herself at Jesus, which may lead us to assume she spoke only through the lens of passion. But what if her tears and her words were not only emotionally charged but also evidence she understood the truth about the Messiah? If Peter had done that instead, would we interpret their comments differently?

The two ladies are perfect examples of mindful women of God. Allowing the Holy Spirit to change their minds, they can receive and adopt a new point of view and align with God himself on the matter and love him with all their hearts, souls, *and* minds.

Our Death-Conqueror raised Lazarus from the dead, proving himself to be the resurrection and the life. No doubt Mary, Martha, and Lazarus must have been overjoyed by Christ's miracle. It makes sense that the next time they saw Jesus in Bethany they threw a dinner party in his honor.

Think about sitting next to Lazarus at a dinner party. I wouldn't be able to stop staring. People, he was dead. Then Jesus made him alive. What else is there to talk about with both Lazarus and Jesus present?

At some point during the meal Mary took a pound of expensive oil, worth one year's income, to anoint Jesus's feet, then wiped his feet with her hair (John 12:1–3). Mary appeared three times in the Gospels, and each time we find her at Jesus's feet. The disciples got angry about Mary's wasted treasure and the missed opportunity to help the poor with such a valuable commodity.

But what they failed to recognize was that they are the poor, the spiritually poor. What the disciples judged as a reckless act was just the opposite, according to Jesus. It was the most appropriate response to her Messiah.

I think Mary knew Jesus was the resurrection and the life, and she understood he was going to die. Honoring her King with a burial anointing was not only a courageous act of vulnerability but also a smart move.

Transforming Our Perspective

Loving God with all our minds is a task God calls both men and women to pursue. It exceeds receiving the mind of Christ at salvation, taking evil thoughts captive, and replacing them with pure ones. Mindful women of God go one step further. They are open to new ideas and allow God to transform their perspectives. As Paul instructed, "By the mercies of God, I urge you to present your bodies as a living sacrifice, holy and pleasing to God; this is your spiritual worship" (Rom. 12:1 HCSB). Then giving us examples of how to do this, he said, "Do not be conformed to this age, but be transformed by the renewing of your mind" (v. 2 HCSB).

A New View on Race

God has changed my opinions many times since I became a Christian as a teenager, but none have been as tricky as reversing my views on race. Although I am biracial, I look white and adopted all of the privileges that come with my skin color. If you had asked me about racism a few years ago, I would have proudly told you I was color-blind—while waving my hands in the air as if to swat away the topic. I would have said, "I judge all people as we all should, by merit." Then, I would quickly redirect the conversation. The number of seconds I would willingly discuss race represented how necessary I thought the topic was.

My *mom* is brown.

I *love* my black friends.

I *have* black friends.

I used to explain racism as something that happened in the past through the personal sin of uneducated and backward-thinking people. All these things are right, yet insufficient. Racism isn't distant or past. It is not only individual sin but also communal. Until very recently, I didn't understand how my skin color had anything to do with my identity. I could imagine, but not name, systems of oppression for people of color. But I was convinced the civil rights movement had buried those cycles.

It shocked me to hear a friend of color express concern about the racism in Dallas. Shaking my head in disagreement, I responded with, "Nooo." *No. This is my city. I know and love my city. We are not racists here.* But as my awareness increased, my mind started to change. Listening to the experiences of my friends of color in predominantly white spaces, I began to realize that the fears they have for their dark-skinned children are not the same as mine for Caleb. I do not worry about my son walking down the street to the gas station with a hoodie on or getting stopped by a police officer because he doesn't look like he belongs in our predominantly white neighborhood.

Weeks later I returned to my friend who expressed concern about the racism in our city to apologize for my thoughtless comments. My unawareness echoes a prevailing narrative for many well-intentioned Christians who are like me. According to *Whiteness 101*, a faith-based curriculum from Be the Bridge ministry:

> Conversations surrounding race in America are fraught with contentious rhetoric. On all sides of the issue, there is hurt, distrust, and misunderstanding. White people are often at a disadvantage in discussion about race, because most of us are not fluent in the language of race. For many of us, the few conversations about race we have been a part of were not positive or constructive. . . .
>
> People of color are often shocked to discover that a majority of white people rarely, if ever, talk about race, especially as it relates to their own identity. In other words, we don't often talk about what it means to be white. "Not having to think about our racial identity" is a very white experience. Most people of color are forced to consider their racial identity multiple times a day, every day.[1]

By God's grace, and the seemingly unending patience of my Be the Bridge to Racial Unity small group, the Holy Spirit continues to renew my mind. Sleeping through injustice was dreamy and restful and full of white noise. Awakening to reality, I find myself woefully unprepared to divest my white privileges. I fumble conversations about racial unity with cowardice. And I am fragile about the whole situation because I've been protected and insulated all my life. I have no practice dealing with talk about race, let alone working toward racial unity. While I fear this topic, my friends of color live afraid, period. Having never engaged in a thoughtful conversation about race until adulthood,

NO MORE HOLDING BACK

I realize I used to be unintentionally complicit in participating in racism by never questioning the benefits coming my way.

Becoming a Living Sacrifice

In Romans 12, when the apostle Paul described conforming our brains to God's will, he said we must present our bodies as a living sacrifice—which is a throwback to the Old Testament when priests would kill animals at an altar to symbolize the redemption process. For the Jewish people in the Old Testament, producing purity required a gruesome offering that cost the animals their lives. The apostle Paul was borrowing first-century Christians' familiarity with the sacrificial process to teach them about the new way to live sacrificially in a relationship with Jesus. It means dying to our old reasoning in the same way I am dying to my previous reasoning of racism.

Continuing his exhortation for radical transformation into Christ's image, Paul preached, "Do not conform to the pattern of this world, but be transformed by the renewing of your mind" (Rom. 12:2 NIV). Racism is a pattern of our society, a cycle that continues today, and we are not supposed to participate, benefit from, defend, or ignore it.

In 2008 I cofounded Polished, an outreach ministry to share the gospel with young professional women. Seven years after our inception, I reviewed our Polished speaker lineup, director team, and volunteer roster and discovered we were almost all white. I have built an organization that claims Jesus is Lord without representation from women of color. No, not just representation—I had never even considered women of color. I am not just part of the problem—I *am* the problem. I was not color-blind—I was just blind. And deaf. And dumb. Thank God, Jesus came to heal and save people like me.

Transforming Our Thoughts

Things are changing in my organization—the leaders, the attendees, the topics. Glory to God! We celebrate progress but continue to pursue cultural intelligence with constant intensity. The folks who think I'm just on my newest social-justice-warrior kick underestimate the work of the Holy Spirit empowering me, empowering all of us. We are just getting started.

As executive director, cofounder, and preacher, I used to write myself into our speaking schedule 50 percent of the time. But I'm off the speaking schedule now to make room for my sisters of color. The shift felt radical at the time, and it confused a lot of people. They would remind me that I had worked hard to carve out a space to use my gifts, and I was giving it up to address an issue they did not think existed. No matter what we think about racism, we can all agree that giving away power is always the way of Christ. Although Jesus is God, he condescended to us in bodily form, gave away his life, and left us with the strength of the Holy Spirit. His example is to share and give away power.

I wonder how your understanding of the world around you is undergoing reconstruction today. I know that admitting we are wrong feels like death. When our pre-Christ brain waves interfere with our new lives, it is confusing. Choosing not to conform to prevalent opinions means being a living sacrifice. Without exaggeration, it means laying to rest our old ways of thinking. Awareness is God's grace to us when we want him to teach us new things and change the way we think. Mindful women honor God with their thoughts and their thought processes. And any needed transformation in our thought-lives must begin with the hope of the gospel.

Staying Grounded and Steadfast in Our Faith

We find the key to loving God with all our minds in this passage:

> Once you were alienated and hostile in your minds because
> of your evil actions. But now He has reconciled you by His
> physical body through His death, to present you holy, faultless,
> and blameless before Him—if indeed you remain grounded
> and steadfast in the faith and are not shifted away from the
> hope of the gospel that you heard. (Col. 1:21–23 HCSB)

The hope of the gospel is that we were created in God's image
to flourish and co-create alongside him in the world he breathed
into existence. The hope of the gospel is that even though we
rebelled against God's plan for us, Christ stepped into our mess
to clean it up through his life, death, and resurrection. The hope
of the gospel is that this is not as good as it gets. A day will come
when Jesus will complete the work of restoration that he started.
The hope of the gospel is that God will make all things new, and,
while we wait, we can join him in restoration work.

Steadfastness to these truths filters our logic, rearranges our
priorities, changes our opinions, crucifies old, unregenerate behavior, and keeps our minds open to new ideas. If redemption is an
ongoing process, the redemption of our minds will be too. Women
who love God with all their minds remember that the Holy Spirit
cannot do the work of sanctification—of making us more like
Jesus—unless we welcome his new ideas. Women who love God
with all their minds constantly invite God to have his way in them.

Discussion Questions

- What does awareness look like in your life?
- How could you better love God with your mind?
- What ideals and opinions of the culture around you are you imitating?
- How are you responding to the Holy Spirit's leading you into a new way of thinking?
- With whom could you start a dialogue that might help you in your new way of thinking?
- How could you start a dialogue with someone who might need your help as he or she seeks understanding? What's a good way to prepare yourself for this type of conversation?

NINE

ALL YOUR STRENGTH: SLAYING
THE FORCES OF DARKNESS

> I thank Christ Jesus our Lord, who has given
> me strength to do his work. He considered me
> trustworthy and appointed me to serve him.
>
> —1 TIMOTHY 1:12 NLT

The joy of the Lord is Rocio Lopez's strength; she's a pillar. I recently asked her about her newest job title, because it's hard for me to keep up with her promotions. I think she's the president of the CEO of the director of the leaders. Or something like that. The point is, she does everything with excellence, taking such pride in her work. And she is a strong leader. It's no wonder she keeps getting promoted. But that's not the only reason she is a dynamo. Rocio has weathered the knock-you-down-and-take-you-out storms of life and yet continues trusting in God, her solid Rock.

As the oldest child in the family, and a single woman,

Rocio is her mother's self-appointed primary caretaker. Her caregiving journey began in 2011, when her mother's health started to decline. She never envisioned a life full of doctors' appointments and surgeries for her mother, but ask Rocio to describe her harrowing experience and you'll get pages of praises. God is her Provider, Protector, Good Father, Healer, and Comforter.

My friend Rocio is using everything God has given her, including her business leadership abilities, to benefit her mom in her time of need. It's the clearest picture I have of a godly woman defying the cultural expectations for women to be meek and mild, instead fortifying herself in God's power so that she can be strong for her mom and for herself. Rocio Lopez loves God with all her strength. It's an undeniable outer working of God's power inside of her. She's a warrior for Jesus.

While advocating for her mother, she's had to ask doctors hard questions, challenge their recommendations, and ask for second opinions. At times it felt as though she was bucking the system that says women should be seen and not heard. There's no line she wouldn't cross to save her mom's life. Maybe that's what's missing from our understanding of loving God with all our strength. And maybe we fail to see that the strength she displays at work and at her mother's bedside are both admirable and acceptable ways to bring God glory. They should translate to home, work, church, and everywhere in between.

While Rocio is advocating for and protecting her mom, Jesus is fortifying her in his grace and mercy, which, Rocio says, "Always comes in the perfect dose at the perfect time." Sustaining Rocio and her mom through hepatitis C, liver disease, a liver transplant, and cancer, God keeps proving he will do the heavy lifting for them both. Eighteen months post-transplant, Rocio's mom is healing. Meanwhile, Rocio is testifying that God carried them both through suffering.

I've told Rocio that I wish I could learn to exhibit her strength without having to go through the trials. She gently reminded me that her strength comes from the power of God himself and that power is available to anyone who is a Christ-follower.

When I read Jesus's words in the Great Commandment to love God with all our strength, Rocio is the first person that came to my mind. Maybe you know what Rocio's situation is like. Maybe you're the one in your family who steps in to make sure there is peace, to make sure everyone's needs are met, that everyone is doing okay. Or maybe Rocio's story is too close to home as you care for a sick or elderly parent or because you are facing health struggles yourself.

We might feel comfortable talking about the strength or power of the Lord, but as women, rarely do we feel comfortable talking about our own strength or power that comes from the Lord. But the truth is, God is all powerful, and he gives us his power through the Holy Spirit. And using our power for God's purposes makes us strong. If Jesus instructs all of us to love him with our strength, harnessing God's power to work through us is not only a necessity but an act of surrender to God's priorities.

Jesus has given you the strength to do his work the same way he has given it to Rocio. He considers you trustworthy and has appointed you to serve him (1 Tim. 1:12). Whatever is coming against you this season might be beyond your capacity but not God's. Although serving your King will always include setbacks and obstacles, he knows his divine assignments can be accomplished through you by his own power. Like Rocio, you and I have to harness God's power to develop godly strength so that we can serve God everywhere he has appointed us to serve.

The question on my mind is, How strong is too strong? I'm asking for my *ezer* girlfriends—my women warriors—because there's Boston strong, and Texas strong, and Beyoncé-pregnant-with-twins strong, but there's nothing like the strength of a godly warrior. Nothing. But through experience, we know of the unspoken parameters for women with strong personalities, sharp convictions, prophetic leanings, dynamic leadership skills, or a willingness to speak up. "She's a strong woman" should ascribe honor, not be a warning, and "She's a force to reckon with" should have our enemy running scared.

I used to think Christian men should lead the charge in loving God with all their strength, but even after I started to apply all of the Great Commandment to my life, I wondered how strong is "too strong" for Christian women. Most of us know we can be, should be, and were designed to be strong in the Lord, but where's the line? When did we start assuming strong is an unwanted personality type rather than a level of kingdom-minded commitment?

One day a brother in Christ pulled me aside after a Sunday school teacher meeting, one in which I was the only woman, and pointed out I was not my usual self. I laughed and said, "I wasn't sure I could be." The thing is, folks wonder if women with zealous passion for the Word can also be truly committed to a family or household. Those who show dedication to thinking deeply about the Scriptures are accused of stepping into territory better entrusted to men. Those who speak out against injustice with any hint of anger are labeled as "divisive."

Never mind that our male brothers in Christ who showed zeal, theological understanding, or anger against injustice would be applauded for being tough, godly leaders. It's just not the same for women. And not only for women in the church. Often ladies in the boardroom and workforce confide in me with similar woes. The same traits that make a businessman "successful" make a businesswoman profane. Such patterns incline me, as a woman, to tailor myself to fit my surroundings.

How I serve God used to depend upon who surrounded me at the moment. I found it safer to hide my strength. We risk more showing up with all of ourselves and letting God's power work through us. We waste precious time continually assessing how the space around us will respond to our convictions, but I get our reasoning for holding back when it comes to growing in the strength of the Lord.

Somewhere along the way, we started to believe women are not supposed to be powerful—the result of becoming strong. According to a 2018 Pew Research study, "Americans are much more likely to use *powerful* in a positive way to describe men (67% positive) than women (92% negative)."[1] Maybe it's because we are called the weaker vessel one time in 1 Peter 3:7. Perhaps it's because some men have greater physical strength than women, and strength is not a valued trait for women the way it is for men.[2] Whatever the case may be, the truth is, in God's preferred authority structure, before the fall of mankind, men and women were called to fight forces of evil together. Ladies, gospel work requires fierce soldiers. Our enemy doesn't play nice. He came to kill, steal, and destroy. But we are up to the task because of Jesus.

Raising Your Wakanda Spear

I agree with writer Kathryn Freeman's assessment of the block-buster, record-breaking Marvel movie *Black Panther*, which is set in the fictional African country of Wakanda. She says, "The women in *Black Panther* are the best representation I've seen of God's intention for His daughters. It may be a story, but it speaks a truth that's been long silenced."[3]

My sisters who've seen *Black Panther* know what I am about to say. You and I need to take up our Wakanda spears just like Nakia, Okoye, and Shuri. The Dora Milaje, an all-female military unit enlisted into the Wakandan army, exemplifies what it looks like to defend the king, advance the kingdom, protect the vulnerable, and fight for justice. Interestingly enough, the physical and intellectual power of these leading ladies does not undermine or threaten the men living in Wakanda or the male rulers in power. Instead, those women make everyone better and the country more formidable.

Pastor Thabiti Anyabwile put it this way: "One can be an incredibly strong, competent, and loyal soldier while simultaneously a modest, feminine, beautiful and suitable spouse. Our world does not hold those things together very well. The vision of *Black Panther* holds it together beautifully in Okoye." Okoye, the commander of the Wakanda women warriors, is a heroine worthy of praise: competent, loyal, and fierce. In Anyabwile's opinion, "It's that kind of loyalty from Black women that has quite literally made the survival of Black people in America possible."[4]

Spoiler alert! Bounce your eyes if you haven't seen the movie yet. I left the theater wanting to write a whole book about all the biblical parallels, especially the women at the resurrection. Gathered around the body of King T'Challa, the women first see the good king rise again.

Time and time again I watched the women in this movie hold nothing back as they exhibited strength and used their power for good. I couldn't help but imagine a world in which we celebrated—rewarded, even—women who have no problem correcting the men in their lives, running ahead to catch the bad guys, or taking the lead on initiatives that best suit their expertise. I left the movie emboldened, thinking, *Somebody get my sisters their Wakanda spears, because we are ready to fight!*

You and I are going to face battles that require the efforts of gospel-focused people willing to resist the Devil, the kind of battles we win with the Word of God and through the power of prayer. I raise my crossed arms with my sisters and shout, "Wakanda forever!"

Owning Your Strength

I tend to think of strength in physical terms, but in the 264 times the Hebrew word for *strength* is used in the Old Testament, the majority of the references mean spiritual strength—the strength of the Lord. The Hebrew word can also be explained as "efficiency," "wealth," "army," "warrior," or "influence." It comes from the same root as the verb *chil*, which means "to be strong," or "to be firm."[5] In one rendering, theologians likened the word *strength* in the Old Testament to "using our muchness with force." Now, there's something to rally around.

Biblical language scholars of the New Testament define the Greek word for *strength* as "exceptional capability, with the probable implication of personal potential." They suggest translating the Great Commandment as "Love the Lord your God as completely as you can."[6] Consider the implications such a reading would cause in our willingness to serve God. What talents have you inherited through God's grace? What passions has the Spirit instilled in your heart that would benefit the body of Christ? Are you using them? You are on assignment, sister. For this time, for these people, for this space in history, God has appointed you to those tasks. Called by God, equipped by the Spirit, and compelled by Christ's love, we are supposed to use the fortitude God dispenses with gusto.

Raising Your Hand

"I'll be the last resort," she told me. While the finance committee at her church struggled to find one more strategic numbers guru to add to the existing committee, this young lady, equal in qualifications, experience, and character, did not raise her hand. She was a likely candidate but was choosing to wait and see if any men stepped up to fill the need. Why do we do that? Where in the Scriptures do we find any suggestion that women should be offering themselves as a last resort?

No more hedging our bets, ladies. We need the resolve the apostle Peter described when he said that if Christ's suffering is any indication of what the world will do with people committed to God's upside-down kingdom, we must ready ourselves. Beyond serious and disciplined prayer and intense love for one another, his letter recommends being good managers of the "varied grace of God." It appears Peter was equating prayer and love with stewarding our gifts and talents when he wrote:

> Based on the gift each one has received, use it to serve others, as good managers of the varied grace of God. If anyone speaks, it should be as one who speaks God's words; if anyone serves, it should be from the strength God provides, so that God may be glorified through Jesus Christ in everything. (1 Pet. 4:10–11 HCSB)

If we genuinely believe the God of the universe knit us together in our mother's wombs, orders our days, and handcrafts good works specific for each of us, how can we justify burying our talents?

Peter's convicting words about volunteering ourselves freely is followed by lots of exclamation points: "Be serious! Be alert! Your adversary the Devil is prowling around like a roaring lion, looking for anyone he can devour" (1 Pet. 5:8 HCSB). He continued by reminding Christians to resist the Devil and to be firm in the faith, knowing the God of all grace will alleviate our suffering by restoring, establishing, and—you guessed it— strengthening us (vv. 9–10 HCSB).

The highly esteemed Proverbs 31 woman was clothed in "strength and honor" (v. 25 HCSB). The imagery of dressing ourselves in godly qualities shows up in the New Testament too. An Ephesians 6 woman is to be "strengthened in the Lord and in the strength of his power" (v. 10 NET) by putting on the full armor of God so she would be able to stand against the schemes of the Devil. The passage reminds us that "our struggle is not against flesh and blood, but against the rulers, against the powers, against the world rulers of this darkness, against the spiritual forces of evil in the heavens" (v. 12 NET). In the same way, we are called to take up God's protection so that we are ready to stand our ground. Paul's exhortation ends by clarifying the extent to which women and, of course, men should pursue toughness. He said to do everything possible to stand our ground. Everything.

Before Barneys New York closed for the second time in Dallas, our Polished group hosted a fashion show to raise money for our ministry. Never having attended a fashion show myself, let alone hosted one, I was enthralled by the planning process. It came time to book several volunteers as dressers for the evening—women who would miss the show as they assisted each model backstage with wardrobe changes. Of course, they did get the first look at the styles walking down the runway and made the show more engaging by maintaining the timing of each model.

I'm concerned we picture ourselves helping our brothers put on the armor of God like fashion show dressers instead of envisioning how we, too, muster up as part of God's army. In short, he designed us to be warrior-strong, and we should own it. Our world needs more people willing to confront corruption, resist greed, and wrangle rumors. We need rooms overflowing with Christians travailing in prayer and pushing back the darkness. And we can't accomplish this if we are worried about being "too strong."

Receiving God's Strength

For those choosing to join the front lines of kingdom work, you can do so with great confidence. Ephesians 6:14–17 says that God has surrounded us with himself to fight the good fight. We have the belt of truth. Righteousness guards our chests. Our sandaled feet ready us for the gospel of peace. Our shields of faith will extinguish any fiery arrows launched at us. And we wear the helmet of salvation and carry the sword of the Spirit, his Word. We are battle ready. And we will slay the enemy and his evil army.

Even those of us "leading with a limp"[7] can take up our crosses based on the prophet Isaiah's words. He wrote:

> Do you not know?
> Have you not heard?
> Yahweh is the everlasting God,
> the Creator of the whole earth.
> He never grows faint or weary;
> there is no limit to His understanding.
> He gives strength to the weary
> and strengthens the powerless. (Isa. 40:28–29 HCSB)

Unsure if we can go on one more day, stay committed to our faith, or stand up to the bullies antagonizing us, we don't need just the grit of perseverance. We need the power of someone who never grows weak or tired. Thank God, he shares his might with us. To all those feeling as if they have no say in the matter, no sway in the trajectory, no place in history, the Bible says otherwise.

King David wrote a lyric that speaks to this. He said, "The LORD gives His people strength; the LORD blesses His people with peace" (Ps. 29:11 HCSB). He sure does. Notice that David did not say, "The LORD gives His male disciples strength; the LORD blesses His female followers with peace." David doesn't say, "The God of Israel gives power and strength to his sons." No. God gives strength and power to all of his people.

Finding Your Force

Maybe you just need to hear it. There's no such thing as "too strong" for Jesus-women. We can't be "too filled" with the Holy Spirit. If I went through Paul's list of spiritual gifts in Romans 12, it would serve as a reminder that you can't be too good at prophesying, serving, teaching, exhorting, giving, leading, or showing mercy, and you can't have too much faith (Rom. 12:3–8). If I went through Paul's list of spiritual gifts in 1 Corinthians 12, it would serve as a reminder that you can't display too much wisdom or knowledge, heal too many people, perform too many miracles, or interpret too many languages (1 Cor. 12:8–10). We can't outshine God's glory by showing off his gifts in us.

Author Marianne Williamson expresses it best when she says:

> Our deepest fear is not that we are inadequate. Our deepest fear is that we are powerful beyond measure. It is our light, not our darkness, that frightens us most. We ask ourselves, "Who am I to be brilliant, gorgeous, talented, and famous?" Actually, who are you not to be? You are a child of God. Your playing small does not serve the world. There is nothing enlightened about shrinking so that people won't feel insecure around you. We were born to make manifest the glory of God that is within us. It's not just in some of us; it's in all of us. And when we let our own light shine, we unconsciously give other people permission to do the same. As we are liberated from our own fear, our presence automatically liberates others.[8]

I look forward to a day when women refuse to struggle with this. Capable and tenacious women of God are not less able to parent, submit to authority, serve in the local church, or support a spouse. Powerful Jesus-women in no way diminish the calling, position, reach, or authority of our leaders, pastors, or elders. Our culture may not value powerful women, but Jesus does.

Let's find our power in his presence, our force travailing in prayer, our stance in his sacrifice, and our might in his victory. "She's a strong woman" should be a compliment, not a warning, in our faith communities, because God gives strength and power to all his people. None of us can be too strong in the Lord.

It's the difference between thinking we need to simmer down and knowing we need to power up. In Jesus's name, let's power up.

Now, go and love God with all your strength, because Jesus tells us so. And bring your Wakanda spear.

Discussion Questions

- How strong is too strong for a Jesus-follower?
- What does strength look like for a Christian?
- Who is the strongest female Christian role model in your life? How does she exhibit strength?
- What is holding you back from growing in strength?

PART THREE

THE CALL
TO SHARE
GOD'S LOVE

POURING LOVE OUT

> The second is: Love your neighbor as yourself.
> There is no other command greater than these.
>
> —MARK 12:31 HCSB

L iving and working in the buckle of the Bible Belt had me fooled. As a skin care and makeup sales rep, my largest target market was fast emerging as young professional women, and I mistakenly assumed conversations with them would lead to swapping our spiritual testimonies. Those unrealistic expectations were dashed really fast. At the end of my sales pitch, when I disclosed my intentions to leave my job for ministry, imaginary record players would come to a screeching halt. On a few occasions my faith in Christ invoked profanity and teasing from some customers, but most often just deer-in-the-headlights confusion.

One customer followed the conversation by asking if I was going to be a priest, could I do funerals, and would I have to get divorced to join a church staff? She then proceeded to treat our time like a confessional session, admitting she was stealing from

143

her company and sleeping with her boss, before breaking down into a puddle of mascara. Maybe for the first time, I realized I had neighbors, people around me, who didn't know the love of the heavenly Father, and I wanted to share his love with them.

Extremely motivated, I started inviting women within earshot to join me at church on Sundays or for Bible studies at my home. But the answer was almost always no. Most hadn't stepped foot in church since high school, many had vivid stories to share about their rotten experiences, and a vast majority thought it would be really weird to show up to some random person's home and hang out with her Bible-reading friends. I found loving my neighbors much harder than I'd anticipated. As a healthy coping mechanism, I confided in one of the smartest godly working women I knew at the time, Stephanie Giddens.

Dressed in pencil skirts and button-down shirts, Steph and I would meet up on a regular basis to steep our tea or swirl our coffee and talk about real life and our visions for the future. It wasn't free counseling, but it was a close second. We shared a passion for reaching disconnected and lost women in our generation, and we started to pray weekly about ways we could minister to our coworkers and friends. But we were facing our own set of challenges too.

Balancing career, coursework, and social life, neither of us could attend the women's Bible studies offered at our churches, because we were working during the day and sometimes into the early evening with our classwork. With so little margin, connecting with mentors felt nearly impossible. I wish I could say I was living for the weekends, but the reality was I was living to get my homework done. The only real break we had each day was for lunch, if we were lucky enough to work one in.

In May 2008, Stephanie and I met at Starbucks, as usual, and before I could get in my drink order she put her fist on the table and said, "Kat, let's do something." I told her she had me at hello, then asked what she had in mind. But it didn't matter, because if Steph has an idea, I huddle up to listen to her call a play.

That day she invited me into her innovative dream-building and we turned our venting into brainstorming and our felt needs into a platform. We also asked ourselves many questions. How could we gather young professional women together? Who was already leading discussions on how to navigate a career as young women? How do you explore faith with people who feel disconnected from God and from a local church? How could we show this next generation that the Scriptures are still relevant to our everyday lives? How could we meet them where they are during their availability?

The answer was Polished, an organization we cofounded to become the avenue for outreach to an underserved group, our peers, although back then it didn't have a name. It was just the prayer request we kept bringing up to our small groups. A year after our Starbucks meeting, we hosted our first sixty-minute networking luncheon with a handful of twenty- and thirtysomethings. The event schedule allowed for time to meet new friends, network over the meal, hear the testimony of professional women, and present the gospel to our seekers. It was everything we were looking for in a space tailored to meet our needs and the needs of our peers.

The results have been nothing short of God's grace. Hundreds of events later, we are watching this movement spread across the nation with local chapters and podcast episodes, reaching tens of thousands of career women with the good news of Jesus. Partnering with local churches and likeminded individuals, Polished is building a community for the unchurched, dechurched, and overchurched young professional ladies in our world.

What if our deepest longings are the beginnings of an outreach ministry to people who share our yearnings? Sometimes our own unmet needs are supposed to catapult us into creating something for others as well as ourselves. If necessity is the mother of invention, our heart cries should birth new ministries. Because after Jesus instructs us to love God with all our hearts, souls, minds, and strength, he says to "love your neighbor as yourself" (Mark 12:31 HCSB). It's as if our lives will bubble over with love so that we can impact the people around us.

A New Spiritual Landscape

For thousands of years, the daughters of the church have been invested in kingdom work with sincere determination. We see the fruit of their faithfulness all over the globe. This should be no surprise. Our faith history is rich with radical concepts elevating women as reflections of God himself, and the Scriptures are full of revolutionary female figures that founded, funded, or led alongside their brothers in the birth of the church. Women making a difference for Christ is not a new concept and not one we will ever lose. But the spiritual landscape has shifted. When it comes to our involvement in the American church, we are losing women. And we need to win them back.

Although I am a young woman myself, I hope my voice will always be used to speak for the younger people underrepresented in our communities of faith. The fire I feel in my belly for the next generation rises up and daily brings me to my knees. All my chips are in. Some would label me a "lifer" for these "youngers" (as I like to call them), and that would be fair. But I'd prefer to see my passion as an inescapable result of following Christ. We've seen the Cross, and it demands our life. Speaking for the voiceless is our mission. So it is on behalf of the women who have left our churches that I'm standing at the gate, calling our attention to our sisters who need us.

Women used to be the church's backbone, but now, disillusioned and disenfranchised, we are leaving the pews at record speed.[1] To be clear, the departure is not because youngers are "snowflakes," lazy, or selfish. That story is tired and offensive to those proven to work shoulder to shoulder alongside their elders. The next generation of women values integrity above duty to the church. They have found Christians to be hypocritical, like all generations before them, but they refuse to overlook the lack of consistency in our faith and practice.

The church is more than just an organization, and we will come back to that. But for now, I applaud the character of anyone relentlessly pursuing justice. They will press us on matters of integrity and quickly point out when our words and actions do not align. I welcome their reproof; I've learned over the years they speak up for righteousness if we would only listen.

Let's retire the script that insinuates millennials, Gen X, and Gen Y are slothful dreamers. Instead, we should invite women missing from our congregations into a conversation about why they've chosen to leave, pleading our case for their involvement, because they are a part of the body whether they recognize it or not.

We've been on a trajectory in the United States, one riddled with religious decline for both men and women. For instance, 59 percent of millennials who grew up in church have dropped out at some point,[2] and spiritual but religiously unaffiliated millennials are becoming more and more secular.[3] The Christian share of the US population is declining, while the number of US adults who do not identify with any organized religion is growing.[4]

Skeptics today are, on average, younger than in the past[5] and have a lack of institutional trust that rivals their parents'.[6] Millennials are spiritual but not religious and choose not to go to church because of wounds or because it seems irrelevant.[7] But why is that? Perhaps the most significant transition of all occurred with the entry of millions of women into the skeptic ranks.[8] Almost half of the women surveyed (43 percent, to be exact) feel zero emotional support from their local churches.[9] Let that sink in for a moment.

The only religious behavior that increased among women in the last twenty years was becoming unchurched. That rose a startling 17 percent—among the most substantial drops in church attachment identified in the research.[10] Fewer women experience a traditional nuclear family: they are delaying marriage, choosing to have fewer children, and staying in the workforce longer.[11] In fact, more women are obtaining advanced educational degrees than men.[12]

Reflect on your own tradition. Do the women attending your church mirror what is happening in our society at large? Are female leaders around you attuned to this new reality? And if your lead pastor or elders knew about this, would it surprise them?

The stats are hard to accept, mainly because women's

ministries at church typically thrive with more involvement than do the men's ministries (if they even have a men's ministry). We look around inside and neglect the outsider. We see familiar faces and so easily forget who is missing from the picture.

Together we must face this problem bravely in spite of a temptation to defend our good work up until now. Admitting that our kingdom efforts must improve is the first step. We must consider anything we can do to reach more with the gospel as we contextualize the saving message of Jesus.

The good news is that the next generation has proven to be the most willing to share the gospel, statistically speaking.[13]

Tag, You're It

My friend Valerie knew early on that her ministry to refugees in Dallas would eventually lead her to an overseas mission field. She could have lived anywhere in our city, but she chose a location in the middle of town populated by thousands of refugees. She considered her address a sacred opportunity. Opening her apartment before and after school for the children in her neighborhood became normal, everyday life. The whole complex knew her kindness. Filling out legal documents, making breakfast for hungry kiddos, and giving rides to her neighbors turned into a full-time job.

When she told us about a trip she had planned to an undisclosed location in the Middle East, my husband and I placed bets on how long we thought it would take before she committed to long-term missions in one of the most dangerous parts of the world. As predicted, the Lord assigned Valerie to a place she was not welcome, so she could introduce women to her Savior. Anyone who knows her could testify that she was made for this risk.

Aaron and I would joke about not lasting a few days in her shoes, listing all the reasons we would never do something like she did. But for Valerie, this was the natural next step—or I should say—it was the supernatural mission designed for her. Cheerfully supporting Valerie is a reward in itself, but a by-product has been learning about the process future missionaries go through before they arrive in the field.

We found that missionary preparations include rapidly becoming debt free, raising financial support, and selling state-side possessions. Debt-free living sounds like a pipe dream to most Gen Xers and millennials as they carry more educational debt than any of the college-educated people before them.[14]

New missionaries also prepare by finding housing overseas, uprooting the kids if they have children, and enrolling them in new schools in places with fewer options and resources for any special needs. Valerie described cultural-awareness training that sometimes includes role-play through traumatic and life-threatening scenarios. Her training included being taken captive with a bag over her head and being questioned by fake authorities. Say what?

She spent weeks timing immunizations. Her to-do list included researching customs regulations and packing her belongings. Valerie would learn to live in more than one-hundred-degree heat while covering her whole body from head to toe. In that country she could no longer look directly at men or even be in their presence. The changes were drastic. But the big one was starting over: new place, new friends, new language, new *everything*. The huge barriers to entry were astounding.

In contrast, most of us face few obstacles to access what *Christianity Today* has called "the newest US mission field": women.[15] We already speak the language; we don't have to leave our homes, pack or sell our belongings, find a new place to live, or go through the hassle of getting to know new neighbors. We are best equipped to reach the women exiting the faith. That means I am, and you are, the missionaries God is sending.

What if the angst we sense in disillusioned Christians has less to do with what the church is doing or not doing on their behalf and more about us actually being the church? What if we are the answer to their prayers?

Qualified Ministers of the Gospel

After explaining the hardships and rewards of Christian ministry, the apostle Paul asked a witty rhetorical question in his second letter to the Christians living in Corinth: "And who is competent for this?" (2 Cor. 2:16 HCSB). And the resounding response should be "No one." No one is qualified to share the gospel, except by the power of the Holy Spirit.

Just verses later, Paul explained that he is a competent minister of the gospel because of the resurrection power of God that has anointed and sealed and filled him through the Holy Spirit. Sometimes that word *competent* is translated as "adequate, enough, sufficient in ability, or a good fit."

In other words, you are adequate to tell our sisters the truth, you are enough of a Christian to win souls and influence people, you are sufficient in your ability to articulate the gospel, and you are the right fit for the job because you are occupied by the Holy Spirit. You are precisely what our world needs. And your time is now.

How about this? Look up from your desk and zero in on the intern and ask her to lunch. It's just lunch. You don't have to stay up all night writing your own theological thesis or Bible study curriculum to share your life. That intern will spin out in fangirl emoticons that you reached out in the first place. Or walk outside and knock on the door of the youngest woman on your block or hall and ask her over for a cup of coffee. Or leave the comfort of your peers to find the youngest woman in the room, then point her to the cross and empty tomb. Just try it. It's that simple.

Everyone Should Feel This Loved

While my dad was in the ICU following his suicide attempt, a cooler sat on our porch and a key under the mat for weeks as caring Christians made sure we always had plenty of comforting food to sustain our weary bodies. Our water heater burst the day before the service, and a friend reached out to say she had researched the cost of a new water heater and found her bonus was the exact amount we would need. We had hot showers on some of the most trying days because of her generosity.

Next thing I knew, two gentlemen from our church were installing the new appliance and trying to do so quietly so I could rest. I could hear them whispering, "Let's do this right the first time and with one push so she can sleep longer." I found them scrubbing our floors on their hands and knees because it was pouring down rain and they had accidentally brought in mud on their shoes.

I remember my mother- and sister-in-law caring for my son, Caleb, when he came down with strep throat and shielding him from the stress of Pop's passing. I remember the ICU nurses commenting on the people from our church coming to the hospital to pray over the doctors, nurses, my dad's room, even when we were not there. I remember Sarah babysitting several times and dropping everything she had to do to help me. I remember my bestie Lee buying me a funeral dress and explaining to me that I'd never want to wear that thing again. I remember Pastor Brian hugging me with compassion before I walked into a reception overflowing with food and flowers. It must have taken an army to arrange an event that displayed so much care.

The day after my dad's memorial service, I woke up with a splitting migraine, body aches, and dark circles below my puffy eyes. But my heart was full of gratitude. Our community of faith gave us the gift of their love, and the only words I could get out to Aaron on day one post-funeral was, "Everyone should feel this loved, everyone!" When I needed her most, the church showed up for us.

Even now I am flooded with feelings of inexpressible thanksgiving. I began to wonder if our proximity, the tethering we have to a local church because my husband is the pastor, is the primary reason we were loved so well. Because if trends continue and empty pews increase, how will the next generation of women know the tangible presence of God's love through his people? How can we love well if they don't show up?

I think the solution has to come from two directions. One, we need to go out and meet women where they are, wherever they may be, as the messengers God has appointed. *And* unplugged women need to come home to the local church.

You and I can't love others or love ourselves the way Christ envisioned without a tie to a local church community. There, I said it. You may say, "But look at all her crazy." Trust me, sister, I see. Sometimes she's a mess. You may tell me you've found good, trustworthy friends outside the church, and I will celebrate this provision with you. But we need grace well beyond friendship. Breaking bread and drinking the cup, watching the water pour over a new Christian is what bonds us, unites us, in our covenant relationship with the one true living God.

The church is worth fighting for, worth showing up for, because our association with her is rooted in our identity as Christ-followers. Jesus loves her enough to leave the Father's side to die for her, enough to raise to new life and commission her people and empower them with his presence. His longsuffering commitment to the institution is the most important reason we, too, should stay with her. Jesus is with her now, and so we stick with her following his example.

I know it seems counterintuitive to invest in a broken system, but that's exactly what we must do. If you feel let down by the sisterhood of Christian women, I'm sure she has some improving to do. But I also wonder if we're missing *your* voice and can't see our blind spots. The underrepresented voices, underserved demographics, and overlooked needs can and should be met by the body of Christ. I think we may need your help to do it, which is asking a lot. I guess I'm asking you to do for the church what Christ did for her. You know who is best suited to reach women? You are. The Spirit of God has made us competent ministers of the gospel so that we can love others as the missionary God's commissioned.

To anyone wondering if we miss you, we do. Our eyes are on

the road like the prodigal son's father. Your connection to a local church very well could determine her effectiveness in reaching more women with the gospel. In other words, without you, a part of the body of Christ, we cannot fulfill Jesus's second priority: love our neighbors. So come home. Bring your whole self, raise your hand, speak up, and let's watch the Holy Spirit change the body of Christ from the inside out. We belong together.

Audry's cousin invited her to Polished six years ago. She started attending regularly until she hit a rough patch in life. I can remember several times watching Audry wipe away tears during our luncheons and give out big hugs to her table leaders. We knew our ministry was making a huge impact in her life, but then she kind of fell off the face of the planet. We didn't see her for almost an entire year. Little did we know she was battling depression, struggling to get out of bed each day. Apparently an e-mail from us during her hiatus gave her the strength to carry on one more day, and after a long hiatus she made it out to a Polished event. She left our gathering and within just a few hours applied to be a volunteer leader with our organization.

So much had changed for Audry over the last six years—I wanted to grab lunch and get the scoop on her leadership application. She spent most of our meal wiping away tears of gratitude for Polished, as it was many times "the only bright part of her week." She knew when she walked in that room she was "totally accepted." She said, "Polished saved my life." I sat stunned by her admission. Jesus had saved her life through his unconditional love, and now she wanted to pour out the love she was receiving from him and share it with the women in her sphere of influence.

That's exactly what Christ was envisioning for us when he proclaimed commitment to God would mean giving of ourselves fully to love God *and* to pour that love out to others.

Discussion Questions

- Are you connected to a local church? Why or why not? If not, what are some ways you might get connected?
- How could the church better encourage and equip people of this generation?
- Do you feel like a competent minister of the gospel? Why or why not?
- Who is God calling you to love in this season?
- How do you plan to be intentional with those women God has brought to your mind?
- What woman has reached out to you and shown you intentional love when you were in a low season? How can you pay that forward?

ELEVEN

LETTING LOVE IN

> Do not take revenge or bear a grudge against members of your community, but love your neighbor as yourself; I am Yahweh.
>
> —LEVITICUS 19:18 HCSB

There's not much I like more than speaking at youth events. Unrestrained by cynicism, the hope and energy of that age group is contagious. Plus, the music set is always, as kids say, "lit." It totally lights me up too! I'll take sore calf muscles from jumping up and down during a youth retreat any day.

One summer camp where I was speaking, I was welcomed by one of the campers, an exuberant fourteen-year-old girl attending with her youth group. This young lady rolled out a red carpet for me emotionally. She made sure I felt comfortable, asked if I needed anything to drink, and told me she was praying for my message that evening. She wasn't the speaker keeper; she was just kind. After my session, I resumed my position seated in the back row of the dimly lit worship center and bowed my head one last time. Her sweet voice whispered in my ear; she needed someone to talk to. The message had pierced her heart, especially when I shared about my dad's taking his own life and the reasons we choose to stay here on earth, how to find help when we need it, and the One to turn to in the face of crippling fear: Jesus.

It had been ten days since the last time she cut herself. By the time camp was over, the two-week milestone would be within her grasp. The progress felt like freedom but scared her to death. She described piercing herself until she drew blood, watching the cut heal, then wanting to do it again. The pattern had been going on for years. Her parents knew she was struggling, so she was in counseling already. Her spiritual leaders kept tabs on the matter, and everyone was praying for her inner healing, but she felt alone in her pain.

How is it that someone so vivacious, outgoing, and welcoming feels isolated at school, bullied by other girls, and beaten down by depression? I asked her if she loved herself, and she said, "I don't even like me." I asked her if she was a good friend to others and she was amused by the question. She was the best. I affirmed I knew this must be true based on the way she treated me, a stranger.

Moments later she was scooped up by one of the youth leaders, and with that, was wrapped in Jesus's love. A steadfast prayer warrior, this spiritual mother started fighting on behalf of our younger sister in the faith with words that breathed life into the teenager. I was so moved by the experience I ended up struggling to see the dirt roads leading me back home that night because of the constant stream of tears falling into my lap.

It got me thinking about the sacrificial ways we befriend people, knowing it is the way of Christ. And I had to wrestle with the cognitive dissonance of accepting that while we are conduits for God's affection, we resist it for ourselves. Purging, bingeing, cutting, or any type of self-harm is a form of revenge, which leads us to Jesus's instruction to personalize his love. He lifted it right out of Leviticus.

Priestly Stuff: Enjoying a Relationship with God

Reading Leviticus, an Old Testament book of the Bible, is like brow maintenance. Booking your threading technician or waxing specialist, you know it has to be done, although it might be uncomfortable, even painful. But the eyebrow shapes the whole face. Priorities. Similarly, Jesus's chief goals for us to love God and love others require understanding the text in Leviticus, a challenging but vital foundation to our faith.

I'd personally enjoy this Old Testament book better if it had a different title, because right now it sounds like the proper name of a sautéed mushroom, or maybe a cruel medieval king. Purely for concentration, I've used a pencil to cross out the word *Leviticus* in the table of contents of my study Bibles. The new and improved heading, by way of a note in the margin, is "Priestly Stuff." After all, this section of Scripture instructs the priests how to implement God's laws so the people of God could enjoy communion with him.

To be clear, salvation never depends on any kind of ritual because Christian salvation comes by faith in Christ, through

God's grace. What the Lord's ancient laws do is bring us near to God to delight in his presence and savor his blessings. A good subtitle for the book of Priestly Stuff would be "Enjoying a Relationship with God." The book is "primarily instructive history"[1] that emphasizes God's holiness and the corresponding consecration of the Jews who wanted to benefit from a covenant connection with the Almighty.

It's easy to get distracted from Leviticus's purpose, enjoying access to God, once you get into the holiness code in the middle of the book. All the blood and animal sacrifices are foreign. I'm tempted to skip ahead to the New Testament book of Hebrews to hurry up and get to Jesus, the fulfillment of the law. Forget all these cumbersome and impossible-to-meet requirements; give me Jesus. He is the ultimate Priest, and his sacrifice was the final ritual needed to satisfy God's demands. As the writer of Hebrews wrote, "Since we have a great high priest who has passed through the heavens—Jesus the Son of God—let us hold fast to the confession" (Heb. 4:14 HCSB). That's more like it.

I prefer to focus on the fact that now all Christ-followers are a nation of priests. According to the apostle Peter:

> You are a chosen race, a royal priesthood,
> a holy nation, a people for His possession,
> so that you may proclaim the praises
> of the One who called you out of darkness
> into His marvelous light. (1 Peter 2:9 HCSB)

But then I'd miss the big point of illuminating history in Leviticus and the original context of the Great Commandments.

The Second Greatest Commandment

My licensed professional counselor is a treasure. She has a way of circling back to a topic that surfaces in many of our conversations without a hint of exasperation. So what is it we keep circling back to? How much God truly loves us. She says that intentionally putting the needs of others ahead of ourselves is a lot easier than what goes hand in hand with it—internally absorbing God's enduring love.

Why does it feel icky as a Christian woman to embrace this truth? When I asked my trusted friends how they love themselves, most cringed. All of us expressed, in one way or another, that self-love seems too close to being selfish. One of my nearest and dearest friends joked, "Let's talk about self-care or self-acceptance. I've got plenty of tips for that." Ditto.

Self-care is all the rage these days. Excusing away a pedicure or retail therapy trip in the name of wellness has become the self-justification I always dreamed of. In fact, I satisfy my impulses so well under the auspices of "self-care" that I am tempted to confuse Jesus's directive to love ourselves as yet more evidence that I need another romper from Anthropologie. Jesus is all for taking care of our minds and bodies. Everybody needs to take a breath, go on vacation, unplug, and enjoy a sweet treat here and there, but Jesus offers us even more.

Speaking to the graduate students at Stanford Business School, Oprah Winfrey answered the question, "Why is it so important to take care of yourself?" She answered by saying that we don't have anything to give that we don't already have. So we must keep our own selves full because that's our job.[2] Hard pass. Listen, I'm going to keep getting her magazine every month, and I appreciate the conventional wisdom she has to offer, but on this we differ. She suggests we have to work hard to keep our cup full. She admits she used to be afraid of folks accusing her of being "too full of herself," but now she wears that indictment like a badge of honor. From her perspective, the only way to be able to offer anything to others is from the overflow of our own capacity. I disagree. In the absence of confidence, compassion, patience, or kindness, I believe we can draw from the deep well of our Savior's abundance.

Some commentators list the verses in Leviticus 19 as miscellaneous. I find that fascinating. Smack-dab in the middle of a section of the Bible that often gets lost, has seemingly little order, and feels irrelevant to our modern lives is a verse that would be immortalized as of the utmost importance by our Savior. Jesus quoted part of Leviticus to say love others and love yourself. What does Mark 12:31, the verse about being a good neighbor and having self-compassion, have to do with the holiness codes in Leviticus 19? I think both passages connect the radical, singularly focused love of God to how we let God's unconditional love in.

Internalizing Love

Parenting my five-year-old centers around creating choices. "Caleb, you can finish your dinner and enjoy a dessert, or you can put your plate on the counter and the meal is over." "You can stop crying and enjoy the park, or we can pack up and head home." "You can take a bath now or after your TV show. Which would you prefer?" Parenting also revolves around constant reminders.

Friendly reminders to say "please" and "thank you," "yes ma'am," and "yes sir." Stern reminders to stop harassing the dog. Irritating reminders that yes, of course we have to wear shoes. "Please, please, put on your *shoes!*" When God means business or needs our attention, he also tends to repeat himself.

Caleb had us in stitches when, with his head held high, he responded to one of our suggestions: "I choose not to do that, but thank you." You have to hand it to him; the politeness almost covered up his defiance. We had to tenderly explain that we were not asking him to make a choice; we were telling him to do something. He furrowed his brow and squinted his eyes to communicate this was unsatisfactory. While Caleb is learning our cues, I've noticed my own failure to take some of my Father's words earnestly.

Scripture says, "The LORD spoke to Moses: 'Speak to the entire Israelite community and tell them: Be holy because I, Yahweh your God, am holy'" (Lev. 19:1–2 HCSB). And then for the next few verses God ends most of his instructions by repeating the obvious: "I am Yahweh your God." He says the phrase seven times in chapters 19 and 20:

"I am Yahweh your God."

"I am Yahweh your God."

"I am Yahweh your God."

"I am Yahweh your God."

"I am Yahweh your God."

"I am Yahweh your God."

"I am Yahweh your God."

If we are listening, we cannot miss his point. Self-love is God's business, and he takes it seriously.

Moses continued by including instructions that put the Ten Commandments into practice. He emphasized things like not stealing, not lying, not taking the Lord's name in vain, providing for the vulnerable and the refugee, and using justice and fairness to judge legal cases. Then he prepped us for the verse that would end up in Jesus's Top 2 list: "Do not seek revenge or bear a grudge against anyone among your people, but love your neighbor as yourself. I am the LORD" (Lev. 19:18 NIV).

The same thing shows up in Romans when Paul wrote:

The commandments:

> Do not commit adultery;
> do not murder;
> do not steal;
> do not covet;

and whatever other commandment—all are summed up by this: Love your neighbor as yourself. (Rom. 13:9 HCSB)

Could it be that we are good at treating others the way we want to be treated, but we struggle to love ourselves the way God intended? What if self-love is not selfishness at all? What if it's the opposite of self-hate? I'm imagining freedom, bought by Christ's blood on the cross, used to remove the grudges we hold against the person in the mirror. I'm envisioning our openhandedly accepting redemption as a cherished gift—to us.

Eugene Peterson paraphrased the apostle Paul this way:

It is absolutely clear that God has called you to a free life. Just make sure that you don't use this freedom as an excuse to do whatever you want to do and destroy your freedom. Rather, use your freedom to serve one another in love; that's how freedom grows. For everything we know about God's Word is summed up in a single sentence: Love others as you love yourself. That's an act of true freedom. If you bite and ravage each other, watch out—in no time at all you will be annihilating each other, and where will your precious freedom be then? (Gal. 5:14–15 THE MESSAGE)

Do it for yourself, my friend. Love others without holding back love for yourself.

True Self-Love

Aaron has officiated in more than twenty weddings. On occasion, the bride or groom will express wishes to exclude certain "overused" passages of the Bible in the sermon, things that feel too generic. Usually they choose to chop 1 Corinthians 13, the love chapter. I get what they are saying, but we can't forget the importance of these familiar verses—not only in the context of marriage but as a way to edify Christians into self-love.

If love is patient, we should be patient with ourselves. Why is it we can remain composed when our friends repeat the same mistakes over and over, but when we follow a similar pattern we end up berating ourselves with negative self-talk? Our roommates, coworkers, spouses, and children usually get several chances, loving correction, and ample time to course correct on a myriad of issues. But when it comes to us, we've got a short fuse. It would be revolutionary to see women extend more grace when we are alone with our thoughts, reviewing the events of the day, or simply laugh at mistakes and move on quickly without shame.

If love is kind to others, it should be kind to you too. Many of the things I am allowed to say to myself would ruin friendships if I directed them toward my besties. Sometimes our small inner voice ends up screaming abusive words that cut us down. We would never allow this in normal conversation. Because we know that "kind words bring life, but cruel words crush your spirit" (Prov. 15:4 GNT). I would never say to my loved ones, "That was stupid; I hate your dress; everyone will notice you are out of place today." But I don't flinch when those comments are coming from me to me. Our negative self-talk has to go.

The apostle Paul likely knew the pendulum could swing in the other direction when it comes to loving ourselves. His next comments include denouncing conceit and selfishness. This should debunk any myths about "being full of ourselves" as a means to get ahead or as a natural result of healthy self-confidence. Fulfilling Jesus's goals doesn't come with license to be prideful.

I can't fathom erasing my laundry list of wrongs. Not only do I keep receipts on all the dumb things I've done in life, but when new evidence reveals I have not progressed, I add to my tab of misgivings. But love does not keep a record of wrongs, because God removes our transgressions as far as the east is from the west (Ps. 103:12). Forgetting our sins is God's specialty. Are we bookkeeping our faults? That's not self-love. True love confesses, repents, and accepts Christ's forgiveness. What if we actually started to believe that in addition to wiping everyone else's slates clean, God is doing the same for us? Your slate has been wiped clean, dear one (Col. 2:14).

Friends warned me that in writing a book, a blank page and blinking cursor might catapult me so far away from the truth that I'd land in the quicksand of impostor syndrome (yes, it's a real thing), where people doubt their abilities and are convinced they're phonies. Maybe you have had a touch of it at some point in your career too. Since signing my book deal I've had recurring nightmares about the "just kidding" e-mails from my editor to notify me the signed contract has been rescinded. Persistent feelings of inadequacy created writer's block and kept me awake at night. I have to remind myself that love rejoices in truth—it doesn't wallow in lies.

If my friend Sarah could get paid for all her encouragement, she'd be rich. No milestone goes uncelebrated and no promotion or accomplishment goes unpraised around Sarah. She's the first to point out the Lord has us in this place, and she brings a Confetti Pop the size of your arm to prove it. Her texts drip with assurance: "The Lord has equipped you for this moment." Her Voxer messages are almost exclusively prayers of faith: "We can count on God to carry us through." If you want a conversation with Sarah, prepare to be invigorated. She's mastered the art of cheering people into their callings. If you want to complain about the other shoe eventually falling, anticipate her gracious reminder, "God's got this." And forget about bringing your impostor syndrome into her orbit. She'll turn you right around to face the truth and then suggest a cheese board to lift your spirits.

There's a lesson in her example that I want to follow. What if Sarah's habitual instinct to rejoice in the truth was my default self-talk mode? I often resist and sometimes resent the way

God wired me, but I want to be done with that. Let's link arms together and go a different way. After all, we are all worthy to be loved and to find God's love in the body of Christ. Jesus's vision for women includes loving ourselves well. If we can love God with everything we have and then share that love with others, we must surely not hold back when it comes to loving ourselves. If the truth about our identity in Christ is crystal clear, why not celebrate it and let love in?

Before meeting the fourteen-year-old girl at the youth event and hearing her story, I would have considered letting love into our own lives just a matter of spiritual development. In part that is true, but it's not the full story. Loving ourselves is not just the natural next step in obeying the first and second greatest commandments; it has physical implications on how we treat our bodies too. Internalizing God's unconditional love might literally save your life. No more holding back!

Discussion Questions

- How could you be more patient with yourself?
- What do you repeatedly tell your inner self that would cause your girlfriend to drop you as a friend if you said those words to her?
- How could you be kinder to yourself?
- How do you keep your record of wrongs?
- Why do you think Jesus lifts an obscure verse from Leviticus and repeats it in the second greatest commandment?
- What do you need to stop holding back from today?

WHERE DO YOU GO FROM HERE?

> Go into all the world and preach the gospel to all creation.
>
> —MARK 16:15 NIV

Don't stop. Don't ever stop. Keep going, sister of the faith."

The professor's words rescued me from the messages that were holding me back from applying the Scriptures to my life. I had to endure a seminary student yelling at me to "just stop" in class before I realized I had been misreading the Bible through the lens of gender discrimination. Apparently, the seminary student was guilty of the same misapplication of Scripture, which explains his outburst in class. But my professor wouldn't have it, and he set us both straight.

As you can imagine, the professor won my trust that day, and I chose to take many more of his New Testament Bible exposition classes. You would think that just-stop/don't-stop moment in class would rank as the most memorable but it's not. The most memorable was the day I found Lydia in the book of Acts. The professor breezed through her story and the connection to Paul's letter to the Philippians while I was reeling from the discovery of her presence. It's not lost on me that God's timing is perfect. I needed to find Lydia after I could answer the offended seminary student's question, "Why are you even here?" I needed to remove the barriers set up by our enemy that keep us from going all in with God and serving him everywhere. But once I found Lydia I was emboldened in my faith.

Lydia of Philippi

Lydia founded, funded, hosted, and led the first Christian church in Europe. She made history as the first person on the whole continent of Europe to put her faith in Christ. According to professor Richard S. Ascough, "Without Lydia there may well have been no Philippian Jesus community. She was a key player in Paul's social network—one of the pivotal sisters in the faith."[1] Her story takes up only a few verses in Dr. Luke's book Acts, but she's a biblical example of a wholehearted, soulful, mindful, and strong woman of God that I hope we all aspire to emulate.

A city girl through and through, Lydia hailed from a place called Thyatira (in modern-day Turkey) that specialized in producing purple dye and purple cloth, which was a luxurious textile for the elite and nobles of the time. Think Hermès, Prada, Gucci. Since the city of Thyatira served as the intersection of several major ancient roadways connecting to Pergamum, Sardis, Magnesia, and Smyrna, it served as the hub of commercial trade activity and the epicenter of the textile industry.[2]

At some point mid–first century, she moved from one urban

area to another, migrating from Thyatira to Philippi, a Roman colony. We don't know why she moved or when. But we do know her transition was good for business and that by the time we meet her in the Bible, she had been living there long enough to own a home. Philippi was a large port city in Macedonia used for imports and exports, as the Via Egnatia, the main highway across the country, ran right through the middle of town.[3]

Working in the trade of luxury goods, Lydia was a successful and independent businesswoman, and as a result, she was wealthy. Although it's common for women to own homes in our day and age, it would have been unheard-of in Lydia's culture. Apparently her home was large enough for her own family, and potentially for her employees as well, with room to spare to host the Philippian church and the four visiting preachers who shared the gospel with her. In addition, she had the economic means to bulk purchase her wares and ensure they transported from Thyatira, where they were made, to Philippi, where they were sold.

I used to own a company called Baby Bow Tie. Although direct sales was a large part of our kid-and-pet accessory business, we also had accounts with Neiman Marcus, Nordstrom, Citrus Lane, and more than one hundred specialty boutiques in the United States. On this side of large purchase orders, I can appreciate the cash required for production and the risk involved. As a small-business owner, I constantly worried about getting big orders, and when they came across my desk I would worry about filling them. *Shark Tank* fans probably notice that many of the folks appearing on the hit TV show trying to get a deal are asking for advances to fill purchase orders. The struggle is real.

Lydia was either an exporter-importer of the purple cloth and dye or the sales rep for her own brand placed in Philippi.

I wonder if one of the perks of fashion and retail in the first century included wearing the products. If so, we can picture this *ezer* whisking through downtown draped in glamorous threads fit for a royal warrior.

Like Lydia, my friend Alina is a vision of fashion. Baffled by her seemingly incomparable sense of style, I asked her why her outfits always look put together, and she explained she picked up the tricks of the experts while selling clothes at a high-end retail store in Dallas. Audry's story is similar. She may just be breezing through on her way to run some errands, but she looks like she stepped straight out of a magazine. She worked for years at Neiman Marcus. While trying to help me get dressed, she suggested that I mix my "highs" and "lows," and I was like, "Uh, do they sell 'high and low' at Target?" Little did I know, she meant integrating high-end and low-end pieces. Right.

Before launching a small business in the fashion industry, I didn't know buyers working at retail companies shopped for items in bulk at markets around the world. The first time it was suggested I show my products at the Dallas Market Center, I pictured a foldout table pitched in a church parking lot with handmade goods. My inaugural shuttle ride from the mile-long parking lot into Market was an experience. Thousands of women dressed to the nines were carting suitcases, wearing official name-tag lanyards around their necks, and entering with their buying assistants. I was alone, uncredentialed, and in workout clothes. What did I know? Obviously, Lydia didn't face a mob of eager shoppers fighting for a place on the elevator, but she would have been in the thick of the hustle however she connected with clients.

We don't know if Lydia was divorced or widowed when she got to Philippi, but some scholars assume she was a single mom

WHERE DO YOU GO FROM HERE?

with at least three or four children.[4] We see you, single moms! But it appears she was married at one time and was no longer married when the apostle Paul, Dr. Luke, Timothy, and Silas met her in Acts 16.

Messages Holding Lydia Back

In the Greco-Roman world, someone's identity was "unquestionably embedded in his or her roles within the family," and households in this culture "fell under the authority of the oldest living male relative."[5] The patriarchal society she would have lived through gave men power and women almost none. Women were valued only as much as they were virgins at marriage and able to bear sons after the union. Lydia seems to be an exception in that she doesn't appear to ask the permission of a male relative in her legal or business dealings or in the matter of hosting out-of-town male guests. She would have inevitably been facing the message that she was a commodity, not made in God's image to rule and multiply alongside the men in her life.

When a baby girl was born into the Roman Empire, no gender-reveal parties popped pink confetti-filled balloons. Since girls would grow up and require a marriage dowry and not be able to join the workforce in the family business, they were a liability. That would explain why many Roman daughters were left outside after birth in hopes they would die or be picked up by slave traders. Lydia would have endured the evil message that as a woman she was not as valuable to her community or to her family as a man would have been. Under Emperor Augustus, a perceived population crisis arose due to the awful practices of devaluing women, so new legislation introduced during Lydia's lifetime helped women like her attain some independence despite being unmarried.[6]

For some readers, the sheer fact that Lydia is in the Bible will make this a milestone moment in your life. It was for me. This savvy single mom and church-planting superwoman seemed to counterpunch all the things I was told about women from the Bible. We have proof that God includes his daughter to build the kingdom as we also see her play an instrumental role alongside the apostles. And she seems to have moved past the teachings in her culture that threatened to keep her from fulfilling God's mission in her life.

I can't wait to meet her one day. My first question will be about the lies the enemy tried to communicate to her that almost derailed her ministry. I want to compare notes and show her the stumbling blocks that almost took out women in my generation: women can't be trusted to learn or lead, I don't have a lot to offer, my greatest joy is marriage and my highest calling is motherhood, I am too much to handle, and leading ladies can't fit in supporting roles. I wonder if any of those will resonate with Lydia.

Lydia Meets the Apostles

On the apostle Paul's second major missionary trip, he met Lydia. He had set sail from Troas, a Greek city located in today's Turkey, with three of his buddies, Silas, Timothy, and Luke. When the four men arrived in Europe, their first stop was Philippi, where Lydia was living at the time. They stayed for a few days in the

city, and then on the Sabbath day, Saturday, the guys went outside the city gate by the river, where they thought there was a
place of prayer.

Luke told the story this way:

> A woman named Lydia, a dealer in purple cloth from the city
> of Thyatira, who worshiped God, was listening. The Lord
> opened her heart to pay attention to what was spoken by Paul.
> After she and her household were baptized, she urged us, "If
> you consider me a believer in the Lord, come and stay at my
> house." And she persuaded us. (Acts 16:14–15 HCSB)

Lydia's Call to Love God

Lydia was committed to seeing her family saved, to the founding
of a church community that would meet in her home, and to
using her influence in her city to further the gospel.

Heart

The Lord opened Lydia's heart to understand the gospel
(Acts 16:14). Yes! Of course he did. None of us can understand
the gospel otherwise. And so began Lydia's journey to love God
with all her heart. After hearing the redemption message of
Jesus, Lydia returned home, shared the gospel with her whole
family, and brought them back to the riverside for Paul to baptize
them as a unit. I can't imagine what hardships she must have
faced after coming to faith in Christ or the persecution her family
may have endured, but she didn't lose heart, as we will see by her
continued work in the book of Philippians.

Soul

Although Lydia was not a Christian when she decided to gather up her girlfriends for a spiritual gathering, the Scriptures make it clear that when she met Paul outside the city gates of Philippi, she bore the marks of a pious woman, taking leadership of a group formed for prayer.

What I want to know is how she was able to convince her friends to join her in ritual worship. She didn't *know* the Savior she worshiped yet. Growing spiritually, as Lydia shows us, can mean taking our first steps toward God when we are unsure he exists or cares. Lydia sought God even though she hadn't heard the name Jesus yet. She was a soulful woman of God, praising him before and after her conversion to Christ.

I wish I knew how many times Lydia showed up to that spot beside the water outside her city before Paul came along. And I wonder how many prayer circles her girlfriends attended before their prayers were answered. They probably never conceived of getting in on the ground level of a worldwide revolution. Maybe Lydia just decided week after week to use her day of rest to fill the God-sized hole in her heart. Maybe the gravitational pull toward the things of eternity was the only motivation she needed to round up the people around her. Her invitation was the catalyst for all of her friends and family experiencing the unconditional love of the Father.

Mind

The New Living Translation of Acts 16:14 phrases things a little differently. It reads, "As she listened to us, the Lord opened her heart, and she accepted what Paul was saying." Lydia's listening ears gave her an open mind. She accepted the new information

Paul was giving to her about Jesus, and as a result, God changed her mind to know Christ as Savior. Lydia was an early adopter of the saving message of Jesus Christ, the first Christian on her continent. If Paul had any doubts about women being easily deceived in Philippi, he certainly didn't reveal it. There is no mention of disappointment that a woman received the gift of faith first and no hesitation to entrust her with the gospel.

Strength

After Lydia's whole family was baptized, she persuaded Paul, Silas, Timothy, and Luke to come to her home as guests. "'If you agree that I am a true believer in the Lord,' she said, 'come and stay at my home'" (Acts 16:15 NLT). Luke says she urged them until they all agreed. Sounds like a strong-willed woman to me. Some Bible versions say she "prevailed" upon them. The Greek lexicons define the word *persuade* as to compel by employing force.[7] I'm shaking my head with laughter. Of course she did. She was just exposed to the life-changing news that her sins were forgiven; she had just watched her whole family adopt the truths of Christ and profess faith through the outward expression of baptism. It's not hard to envision Lydia, a strong woman *before* Christ, employing her God-given strength *after* becoming a Christian to compel the evangelists to stay at her home. Lydia was ready to slay the forces of evil.

Lydia's Call to Love Others

Luke interrupted Lydia's story by narrating a sequence of events that eventually led everyone back to Lydia's home, where the first church in Europe launched. A fortune-telling slave girl was getting on Paul's nerves during his stay in Philippi, so he cast out her demons. Her liberation destroyed the income she was producing for her captors, as she could no longer tell fortunes. Furious, the slave owners threw Paul and Silas into jail. A violent earthquake, caused by God, shook everyone's chains loose, setting all the incarcerated free. Realizing their escape would be blamed on him, the jailer decided to take his own life. Paul screamed to the jailer not to hurt himself and ended up leading him to the Lord. Fearing for their lives, Paul, Silas, and the Philippian jailer escaped jail and sought protection at Lydia's house. Their return to home base spoke volumes of their trust in Lydia.

Lydia was the change agent God chose to cofound the Philippian church with Paul. They were partners, coworkers, trusted friends. Her kingdom work so marked our world that years later Paul's letter to the Philippian church revealed that the community started in her home was successful. And we are still reading her story thousands of years later.

Unaware of Lydia's contribution to the movement of God in her city, I used to read the book of Philippians in a radically different way; I didn't see women in the audience. Imagining the male leaders of the church unrolling the scrolled letter from Paul, I pictured only men in the crowd, maybe women on the periphery. Placing Lydia as the central figure in the history of Christianity in Philippi, I now envision the book of Philippians being read aloud in a group of men *and* women, and I picture a classy figure dressed in purple leaning in to hear Paul's letter:

> To all the saints in Christ Jesus who are in Philippi, including the overseers and deacons.

Grace to you and peace from God our Father and the Lord Jesus Christ.

I give thanks to my God for every remembrance of you, always praying with joy for all of you in my every prayer, because of your partnership in the gospel from the first day until now. I am sure of this, that He who started a good work in you will carry it on to completion until the day of Christ Jesus. It is right for me to think this way about all of you, because I have you in my heart, and you are all partners with me in grace, both in my imprisonment and in the defense and establishment of the gospel. For God is my witness, how deeply I miss all of you with the affection of Christ Jesus. And I pray this: that your love will keep on growing in knowledge and every kind of discernment, so that you can approve the things that are superior and can be pure and blameless in the day of Christ, filled with the fruit of righteousness that comes through Jesus Christ to the glory and praise of God. (Phil. 1:1–11 HCSB)

When Paul addressed his letter to the saints living in Philippi who were serving as overseers and deacons in the Philippian church, Lydia would have been among those in his target audience. When Paul prayed for the Philippian Christians with thanksgiving, his appreciation would have stemmed from Lydia's partnership with him in starting this church and leading it together. He was confident that the leaders in Philippi, Lydia included, started a good work that Christ himself would see through to completion. That's why she, along with many others, had a special place in the apostle's heart. They had helped establish the gospel. Imagine Paul praying over Lydia and her partners in ministry, asking that her love would keep growing in knowledge of Christ and in spiritual discernment. It's almost as if Paul is saying: "Don't stop, Lydia. Don't ever stop. Keep going, sister of the faith."

Immortalized by God himself, what once seemed to me to be a hidden figure in church history was actually a leading lady refusing to let anything get in her way of knowing God. Lydia's strong example should give us courage; we are not alone in our pursuit to honor God with our lives. Since the beginning of time and the beginning of the church, women have been showing up to do the work God ordained them to accomplish. Lydia and all the matriarchs of our faith have left us an enduring legacy, a heritage of heroism.

No More Holding Back

We have a choice to make. We can sit another one out on the sidelines, or we can welcome the opportunities afforded to us by Christ's blood. Let's choose to enlist in God's army and ready ourselves for battle. Let's shield ourselves from the remnant of the misogynistic ideologies silencing our voices and limiting our contributions. Let's quash the insecurities scrutinizing our capabilities. And let's do it all for the glory of God the Father, in the name of Jesus, and in the power of the Holy Spirit.

Where do we go from here, you may ask? The answer is simple: anywhere God leads.

ACKNOWLEDGMENTS

I can't estimate how powerful it is to have sheroes of the faith. Who would I be without strong, godly women like Vickie Kraft, Carolyn Custis James, Jackie Roese, or Beth Moore?

Vickie Kraft, the first women's minister at Northwest Bible Church and one of the first women to graduate from Dallas Theological Seminary, has influenced my life profoundly. Imagining whether or not Vickie would approve of my life choices continues to be a guiding force in my life. Thank you, Vickie, for telling me when I was making no sense at all. I miss your tenacity, and I can't wait to be reunited.

Carolyn Custis James, I own all of your books. True story. Your teaching shapes much of my understanding of the Scriptures, and I'm so grateful for your thought-provoking research. Thank you for writing the messages I most need to hear. You probably don't remember my driving you to the airport after a speaking engagement, but it filled my tank. I was running on empty and I needed your voice.

Beth Moore, I'm so thankful you were the first female Bible teacher and preacher I'd ever heard. Your enthusiasm for the Word and your intimacy with Jesus inspire me. Recently, you've bravely spoken out to defend the dignity of women as image bearers of God, and I'm not sure you can comprehend what that means to your sisters in Christ. Thank you for going first. It is not lost on me that your courage comes at a cost.

Jackie Roese, you and Julie Pierce invited me into your home during my season of identity crisis, and you unknowingly became the trailblazers I needed to see preaching. Thank you for asking me to preach at Magdala. I'll never be the same.

Joey Dodson, thank you for hiring me as a youth intern. You gave me my first ministry job, and I am so very grateful. You used to sit down with Ryan and me with your Bible open and challenge us to dig deeper. I'm thankful my first experience working for a church was under your direction. You treated me like an equal, and I started to believe it.

Michelle Attar, thank you for mentoring me. You took a high risk letting me teach the women of Bent Tree Bible Fellowship at the ripe age of twenty-three. Thank you for raising me up. Look what you started.

Ken Fifer, thank you for believing in Polished long before it was reasonable to do so. Without the backing of our home church at the time and your visionary leadership, there would be no Polished. Thank you for launching us.

Sandi Glahn, thank you for being a sounding board and cheerleader for Team Armstrong. I join an army of women convinced your investment in our lives made all the difference. Although I missed your PhD graduation ceremony, just knowing you were walking across that stage was a corporate celebration.

ACKNOWLEDGMENTS

Glenn Kreider, you are a spiritual father to me. Your words break generational curses, and my whole family has benefited. Thank you. Second only to Aaron, you have been the single most supportive man in my personal life and in my ministry endeavors. In 2009 you taught a class—I have no idea which one—and you explained grace. I look into my son's face and wonder what life would look like had I not taken that Wintermester class. Play all the music videos you want, Glenn. But don't stop teaching the basics. When women approach me about entering the seminary, I send them to you first in hopes your inclusion sets the tone for their experience. I'm grateful we are co-laboring together.

Jan Kreider, you pray for me with such perseverance. Thank you for your constant support. We've logged a lot of years swapping prayer requests, and I know it's fueled me when I wanted to give up. We sat together in a pew for a few minutes while Glenn got miked up for a sermon, and I remember asking you what it was like to be married to someone in ministry. Your eyes showed such kindness. I'm grateful I have you to lean on.

To the Polished board of directors, my trusted ministry partners, you are also trusted friends. If we are going to argue about budgets and initiatives and unify around hard-fought vision, there is no one else I'd rather do it with. You make me better. Thank you.

To the Polished volunteers, leaders, and staff, you're the secret sauce. Our team is an embarrassment of riches. I'll never get over how you give faithfully of yourselves to advance the gospel message.

This book would have made my father proud, and not getting to share it with him in person keeps my joy from being complete. I know one day, and then forever, we will get to share in this joy. Until then, I want to say: Thanks, Dad. You wanted this for me more than I wanted it for myself. I love you.

Mom, you're the strongest person I know. You inspire me through your work ethic, intelligence, and compassion. I am so proud to be Noemi's daughter. Your voice of encouragement steadies me when I think I can't do this anymore. I can only hope I grow up to be more like you. Thanks, Mom. I love you.

My nearest and dearest friends, Lee Armstrong, Jenn Jett, Sarah Conner, Sharifa Stevens, and Tiffany Stein, have fueled this project with prayer. I've borrowed Lee's perseverance, Jenn's encouragement, Sarah's faith, Sharifa's courage, and Tiffany's steadfastness. Thank you for lifting up my arms through this project.

I'm so very grateful that my friend Sharon Miller challenged me to steward this message and that Jennie Allen asked me why I was hiding at Camp Well. Your questions started the fire for this project. Thank you.

Shout out to Kelley Mathews, Nika Spaulding, Hailey Bain, and Lindsay Benedetto. You know why.

Jana Burson, you got it. You knew this message could be something meaningful, and I'm so grateful God has called you to discover new voices. You made this possible. Getting an e-mail response back from you is one of the best things that ever happened to me. Thank you for believing in me. Our world would look different if every agent prayed the way you do.

Debbie Wickwire, my ally and advocate, thank you for your patience. This rookie author will never forget your invaluable direction given in the gentlest and kindest way possible. You had faith in me, and I had to borrow it on several occasions. Thank you for making me better. God united us for this project, and I'm grateful we are in this together. You remind me a lot of Jesus; he loved so well.

Meaghan Porter, thank you for seeing me all the way to the finish line. This project is better because you challenged me and refined the message.

To the marketing team at W Publishing, thank you for helping me steward this message.

To the elders, leaders, and members at my home church, Dallas Bible, thank you for loving and serving my family. It's so humbling to receive your love. Aaron and I are still pinching ourselves that we get to do life together with the DBC family.

While writing the book, I found special encouragement from my Adult Bible Fellowship teacher, Brad Cutrell, and his wife, Crystal. Brad, I'm thankful to sit under your teaching. Annie and Pat Mooney, thank you for leading me through Freedom Prayer. I can't believe the healing that took place in those brief moments in the prayer room.

Aaron Armstrong, you kept asking me how you could help me flourish, and your support has changed me. You've taught me what it looks and sounds like to partner with people as they seek to use their gifts for God's glory. There's something indescribable about knowing you're in my corner. When I look over to see if you've got my back, I can hear you shouting: Go for it! The skin you've put in the game for my dreams is nothing short of love. Thank you. #teamarmstrongforever

NOTES

Chapter 1: Women Can't Be Trusted to Learn and Lead

1. Marg Mowczko, "Misogynistic Quotations from Church Fathers and Reformers," Marg Mowczko (website), accessed November 2, 2018, https://margmowczko.com/misogynist-quotes-from-church-fathers/.
2. Tertullian, *De Cultu Feminarum (On the Apparel of Women)*, chap. 1.
3. Thomas Aquinas, *Summa Theologica*, vol. 1, question 92, art. 1, "Reply to Objection 1."
4. Martin Luther, *Commentary on Genesis*, chap. 21, pt. 6, 27b.
5. Augustine, *De Genesi ad Litteram* vol. 9, p. 5.
6. John Piper, *Recovering Biblical Manhood and Womanhood: A Response to Evangelical Feminism* (Wheaton, IL: Crossway Books, 2012), 72–73.
7. Mark Driscoll, *Church Leadership: Explaining the Roles of Jesus, Elders, Deacons, and Members at Mars Hill*, Mars Hill Theology Series (Seattle, WA: Mars Hill Church, 2004).
8. Karla Zazueta, "Mary Magdalene: Repairing Her Portrait of Misconceptions," in *Vindicating the Vixens: Revisiting Sexualized, Vilified, and Marginalized Women of the Bible*, ed. Sandra Glahn (Grand Rapids, MI: Kregel Publications, 2017), 259.
9. Always, "Run Like a Girl," YouTube, published June 26, 2014.

10. "The Magdala Stone: Oldest Carving of the Menorah," Magdala (website), accessed November 6, 2018, https://www.magdala.org /visit/archaeological-park/the-magdala-stone/.

Chapter 2: I Don't Have a Lot to Offer

1. Kat Armstrong (@katarmstrong1), "Eat Your Heart Out, Gal Gadot. There's a New Wonder Woman in Masada," Instagram photo, May 14, 2018, https://www.instagram.com/p/BixNYzuByA2/.
2. Thomas L. Constable, "Dr. Constable's Notes on Mark" (Plano, TX: Sonic Light, 2017), 184, http://planobiblechapel.org/tcon /notes/pdf/mark.pdf.
3. J. R. Edwards, *The Gospel According to Mark* (Grand Rapids, MI: Eerdmans, 2002), 381.
4. Edwards, 381.
5. Scott Sauls, *From Weakness to Strength* (Colorado Springs: David C. Cook, October 2017), 184.
6. Anne Lamott, *Plan B: Further Thoughts on Faith* (New York: Riverhead Books, 2005), 257.

Chapter 3: My Greatest Joy Is Marriage and Highest Calling Is Motherhood

1. Carolyn Custis James, *When Life and Beliefs Collide* (Grand Rapids, MI: Zondervan, 2001), 71.
2. Joy Beth Smith, *Party of One: Truth, Longing, and the Subtle Art of Singleness* (Nashville: Thomas Nelson, 2018), 18.
3. Smith, 35.

Chapter 4: I Am Too Much to Handle

1. Sheryl Sandberg, *Lean In: Women, Work, and the Will to Lead* (New York: Knopf, 2013), 42.
2. Ron Pierce, "Deborah: Only When a Good Man Is Hard to Find?" in *Vindicating the Vixens: Revisiting Sexualized, Vilified, and Marginalized Women of the Bible*, ed. Sandra Glahn (Grand Rapids, MI: Kregel Publications, 2017), 195–96.

3. Sandberg, *Lean In*, 17.

4. James, *When Life and Beliefs Collide*, 50 (see chap. 3, n. 1).

Chapter 5: Leading Ladies Don't
Fit in Supporting Roles

1. James, *When Life and Beliefs Collide*, 184–85 (see chap. 3, n. 1).

2. James, 187.

3. Marg Mowczko, "A Suitable Helper (in Hebrew)," Marg Mowczko (website), March 8, 2010, https://margmowczko.com /a-suitable-helper/. See also James, *When Life and Beliefs Collide*.

4. Carolyn Custis James, *Half the Church: Recapturing God's Global Vision for Women* (Grand Rapids, MI: Zondervan, 2010), 112.

5. Mowczko, "A Suitable Helper."

6. John C. Maxwell, *Leadership 101: Inspirational Quotes & Insights for Leaders* (Tulsa: Honor Books, 1997), 4–5.

Chapter 6: All Your Heart:
Developing a Heart for God

1. "Our Class," Barre3, https://barre3.com/class.

2. F. L. Cross and E. A. Livingstone, eds., *The Oxford Dictionary of the Christian Church*, 3rd ed. (New York: Oxford University Press, 2005), 744.

Chapter 7: All Your Soul: Praising
God When Life Gets Real

1. C. Schultz, "Soul," *Evangelical Dictionary of Biblical Theology* (Grand Rapids, MI: Baker Book House, 1996), 743–44.

2. E. E. Carpenter and P. W. Comfort, *Holman Treasury of Key Bible Words: 200 Greek and 200 Hebrew Words Defined and Explained* (Nashville: Broadman & Holman, 2000), 178.

3. Timothy Ralston, "The Virgin Mary: Reclaiming Our Respect," in *Vindicating the Vixens: Revisiting Sexualized, Vilified, and Marginalized Women of the Bible*, ed. Sandra Glahn (Grand Rapids, MI: Kregel Publications, 2017), 102.

4. Richard Bauckham, *Gospel Women: Studies of the Named Women in the Gospels* (Grand Rapids, MI: Eerdmans, 2002), 55.

Chapter 8: All Your Mind: Staying Open to New Ideas

1. Be the Bridge, *Whiteness 101: Foundational Principles Every White Bridge Builder Needs to Understand* (2017), 6, https://static1.square space.com/static/558850fde4b0892e071e7960/t/5a7b4ea9e2c483 ccb42b9a73/1518030506168/BetheBridge.pdf.

Chapter 9: All Your Strength: Slaying the Forces of Darkness

1. Kristi Walker, Kristin Bialik, and Patrick van Kessel, "Strong Men, Caring Women: How Americans Describe What Society Values (and Doesn't) in Each Gender," Pew Research Center, July 24, 2018, http://www.pewsocialtrends.org/interactives/strong -men-caring-women/.

2. Walker, Bialik, and van Kessel.

3. Kathryn Freeman, "The Role of Black Women in the Church: A Wakandan View of Flourishing," *Christ and Pop Culture* (blog), March 12, 2018, https://christandpopculture.com/the-role-of -black-women-in-the-church-a-wakandan-view-of-flourishing.

4. Thabiti Anyabwile, "The Black Panther as Afrofuturist Womanist Vision," The Front Porch, February 26, 2018, http:// thefrontporch.org/2018/02/the-black-panther-as-afrofuturist -womanist-vision/.

5. Carpenter and Comfort, *Holman Treasury of Key Bible Words*, 182 (see chap. 7, n. 2).

6. J. P. Louw and E. A. Nida, *Greek-English Lexicon of the New Testament: Based on Semantic Domains*, 2nd ed. (New York: United Bible Societies, 1996), 1:675.

7. Dan B. Allender, *Leading with a Limp* (Colorado Springs: WaterBrook Press, 2006).

8. Marianne Williamson, *A Return to Love: Reflections on the*

Principles of a Course in Miracles (New York: HarperCollins, 1992), 190–91.

Chapter 10: Pouring Love Out

1. "20 Years of Surveys Show Key Differences in the Faith of America's Men and Women," Barna, August 1, 2011, https://www .barna.com/research/20-years-of-surveys-show-key-differences-in -the-faith-of-americas-men-and-women/.

2. "Three Spiritual Journeys of Millennials," Barna, June 3, 2013, https://www.barna.com/research/three-spiritual-journeys-of -millennials/.

3. Michael Lipka, "Religious 'Nones' Are Not Only Growing, They're Becoming More Secular," Pew Research Center: *FactTank*, November 11, 2015, http://www.pewresearch.org/fact -tank/2015/11/11/religious-nones-are-not-only-growing-theyre -becoming-more-secular/.

4. Alan Cooperman et al., "America's Changing Religious Landscape," Pew Research Center, May 12, 2015, http://www .pewforum.org/2015/05/12/americas-changing-religious-landscape/.

5. "2015 State of Atheism in America," Barna, March 24, 2015, https://www.barna.com/research/2015-state-of-atheism-in-america/.

6. "Three Major Faith and Culture Trends for 2014," Barna, February 4, 2014, https://www.barna.com/research/three-major -faith-and-culture-trends-for-2014/#.Ut_dHmTnbgG/.

7. Kate Shellnutt, "Just Give Me Jesus: A Closer Look at Christians Who Don't Go to Church," *Christianity Today*, April 7, 2017, https://www.christianitytoday.com/news/2017/april/love-jesus-not -church-barna-spiritual-but-not-religious.html.

8. Barna, "2015 State of Atheism."

9. "Five Factors Changing Women's Relationship with Churches," Barna, June 25, 2015, https://www.barna.com/research/five -factors-changing-womens-relationship-with-churches/.

10. Barna, "20 Years of Surveys."

11. Barna, "Five Factors."

12. Alana Semuels, "Poor Girls Are Leaving Their Brothers Behind," *Atlantic*, November 27, 2017, https://www.theatlantic.com /business/archive/2017/11/gender-education-gap/546677/.
13. "Is Evangelism Going Out of Style?" Barna, December 17, 2013, www.barna.com/research/is-evangelism-going-out-of-style/#.Ur IG1eJdBPF.
14. Abigail J. Hess, "Here's How Much the Average American in Their 20s Has in Student Debt," CNBC: Make It, June 14, 2017, www.cnbc.com/2017/06/14/heres-how-much-the-average -american-in-their-20s-has-in-student-debt.html.
15. Sharon Hodde Miller, "The Newest US Mission Field: Women," *Christianity Today*, August 9, 2011, https://www.christianitytoday .com/women/2011/august/newest-us-mission-field-women.html.

Chapter 11: Letting Love In

1. Tremper Longman III and Raymond B. Dillard, *An Introduction to the Old Testament* (Grand Rapids, MI: Zondervan, 2006), 83.
2. Stanford Graduate School of Business, "Oprah Winfrey: Take Care of Yourself," YouTube, May 21, 2014, https://www.youtube .com/watch?v=kfLGR0KYuys/.

Where Do You Go from Here?

1. Richard S. Ascough, *Lydia: Paul's Cosmopolitan Hostess* (Wilmington, DE: Michael Glazier, 2009), 1.
2. Ascough, 17.
3. Ascough, 22.
4. Ascough, 45.
5. Ascough, 35.
6. Ascough, 43.
7. Walter Bauer, *A Greek–English Lexicon of the New Testament and Other Early Christian Literature*, 3rd ed., ed. Frederick W. Danker (Chicago: University of Chicago Press, 2000), 759.

ABOUT THE AUTHOR

Kat Armstrong was born in Houston, Texas, where the humidity ruins her curls. She is a powerful voice in our generation as an innovative ministry leader and sought-after communicator. Encouraging women to love God and others with their all, Kat teaches the Bible with humor and heart. She is the cofounder and executive director of Polished (polishedonline.org), an organization that gathers young professional women to navigate career and explore faith together. Kat is invested in the lives of women eager to learn about how the Scriptures are relevant to their everyday lives. She has a master's degree in Christian education. She and her husband, Aaron, have been married for fifteen years; live in Dallas with their son, Caleb; and attend Dallas Bible Church, where Aaron serves as the lead pastor.

www.katarmstrong.com

New Video Study for Your Church or Small Group

If you've enjoyed this book, now you can go deeper with the companion video Bible study!

In this six-session study, Kat Armstrong helps you apply the principles in *No More Holding Back* to your life. The study guide includes video notes, group discussion questions, and personal study and reflection materials for in-between sessions.

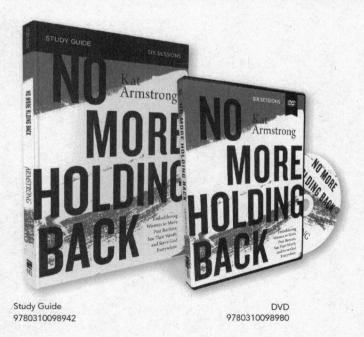

Study Guide
9780310098942

DVD
9780310098980

Available now at your favorite bookstore,
or streaming video on StudyGateway.com.

POLISHED

A network to gather young professional women to navigate career and explore faith together.

Start a chapter in your city for local events
⟶ polishedonline.org/startachapter

Join the online network for discounted ticket prices, digital downloads, and access to our online community
⟶ polishedonline.org/network

polishedonline.org | @polished.online

The Polished Podcast

Hosted by Kat Armstrong

Whether you are multi-tasking or commuting to work, our heartfelt, funny, and fascinating conversations with professional women will encourage and inspire you in your faith and career.

Listen & Subscribe to the Polished Podcast:
polishedonline.org/podcast
available on iTunes